In today's world of  ual
struggle many belie ms.
Dreaming big is ess .... g .... the supernatural realm
and seeing impossible things made possible to see our world transformed as Jesus commanded. In *Dream Wild* Jennifer LeClaire
targets and destroys every mind-set of limitation and inspires us
to work with God to see our wildest dreams come true and our
highest prophetic purpose fulfilled. Get ready to step into an
explosion of possibilities!

—JANE HAMON
SENIOR LEADER, VISION CHURCH AT CHRISTIAN INTERNATIONAL
AUTHOR, *DREAMS AND VISIONS*

This is not a book on interpreting your dreams or visions. Many
Christians can now operate in the dream interpretation grace with
ease, and for that I'm grateful. When it comes to actually dreaming
God-sized dreams, however, many Christ followers are intimidated.
I'm convinced that many people dream short of what's possible
because they settle for vision that can be accomplished through
human strength and ingenuity. We dream comfortable dreams
because we are confident that we can accomplish them through
our own resources and resolve. But there's nothing risky about that.
There's nothing wild about dreaming what you can fulfill through
your own ability. We're OK with dreams that don't scare us. But
Dream Wild is a prophetic call to dream beyond yourself—dream
beyond whatever you could "hope, dream, or imagine" and actually tap into the kinds of dreams that can come to fruition only
through the supernatural power of God.

Dream Wild gives you permission to take the lid off of what's
possible with God. The only ceiling under an open heaven is the
one we build there through our own limited thinking. Through a
very methodical, easy-to-read process, Jennifer LeClaire takes you
through the process of having faith, releasing the Word of the Lord
over your dreams, drawing inspiration from testimonies of other
wild dreamers (I love that!), moving past failure, making healthy
alignments, dealing with doubt, and ultimately taking all the limitations off what God can do.

Jennifer's new book provokes you to see impossibilities as logical.

It makes absolute sense for believers, filled with the Spirit of God—the Spirit who created all things—to dream impossible dreams. Receive *Dream Wild* as your personal prophetic permission slip to imagine the impossible, and cooperate with God Almighty to see what's in heaven released into the earth through your imagination, creativity, and wild dreams!

—LARRY SPARKS, MDIV
PUBLISHER, DESTINY IMAGE
AUTHOR, *BREAKTHROUGH FAITH*;
COAUTHOR, *THE FIRE THAT NEVER SLEEPS*,
WITH MICHAEL L. BROWN AND JOHN KILPATRICK

DREAM
WILD

JENNIFER LECLAIRE

CHARISMA
HOUSE

Most CHARISMA HOUSE BOOK GROUP products are available at special quantity discounts for bulk purchase for sales promotions, premiums, fund-raising, and educational needs. For details, write Charisma House Book Group, 600 Rinehart Road, Lake Mary, Florida 32746, or telephone (407) 333-0600.

DREAM WILD by Jennifer LeClaire
Published by Charisma House
Charisma Media/Charisma House Book Group
600 Rinehart Road
Lake Mary, Florida 32746
www.charismahouse.com

Cover design by Vincent Pirozzi
Design Director: Justin Evans

Visit the author's website at www.jenniferleclaire.org.

Library of Congress Cataloging-in-Publication Data:
An application to register this book for cataloging has been submitted to the Library of Congress.
International Standard Book Number: 978-1-62999-461-1
E-book ISBN: 978-1-62999-462-8

18 19 20 21 22 — 987654321
Printed in the United States of America

This book is dedicated to my dear friends and
co-dreamers in Christ, John and Vanessa Angelini.
You've selflessly helped others pursue their wild dreams.
I pray God makes every single one of your wild
dreams come true for His glory! I love you guys!

CONTENTS

ACKNOWLEDGMENTS

I want to acknowledge all the dreamers who went before me—the daring believers who refused to give up on what God called them to do despite the odds. I appreciate Steve and Joy Strang, who followed God's dream to build a Christian publishing house for His glory. I appreciate Marcos Perez, Debbie Marrie, Maureen Eha, and Adrienne Gaines, the team that dreamed with me to launch a Dream Wild movement that inspires the body of Christ. Thank you for dreaming with God.

FOREWORD

CHRISTIANITY IS THE only religion that dares you to dream wild dreams with God. As a matter of fact, the Bible is full of scriptures that point to two facts:

1. God has deep thoughts about who you are and has things in store for you that are so awesome you cannot even fathom them, as 1 Corinthians 2:8–9 says: "None of the rulers of this age understood it, for if they had, they would not have crucified the Lord of glory. However, as it is written: 'What no eye has seen, what no ear has heard, and what no human mind has conceived'—the things God has prepared for those who love him" (NIV).

2. God wants to give you more than you can hope for or imagine, as we read in Ephesians 3:20–21: "God can do anything, you know—far more than you could ever imagine or guess or request in your wildest dreams!" (THE MESSAGE).

Before God created each one of us, He handcrafted our lives, our destinies, our callings, our personalities, and our passions. He built into you everything you would need to partner with Him to see His fullness manifest in your life. And oh what a fullness He has for you!

Developing a life in God that is conducive to being a dreamer is something you have to pursue and grow in. It is not always natural to our human senses because it requires our relationship with God to bear fruit. So many challenges come up when living this kind of life of faith, so it is more of an earned virtue. I love what Bill Johnson, pastor of Bethel Church in Redding, California, often says: "The Holy Spirit is limited by unbelieving believers." This is so true! We have to grow in our connection to the heart, mind, and thoughts of God through both the Word and His Spirit so we can start believing for His dream!

I remember having an encounter with God in 1996 that caused me to begin dreaming about His heart for the entertainment industry and for Los Angeles. This escalated into a twenty-year spiritual and prophetic journey that in 2006 brought me to LA, where I eventually planted a ministry for creatives and worked with Christians in Hollywood. Now, more than ten years later, it just keeps getting better!

This dream required taking great risks. My family and the ministry I was involved in had no heart for Hollywood, let alone Los Angeles. They even had some bad eschatology toward Southern California. I was not only resisted along the way; I was tempted to lose faith, and I often lost sight of the goal of loving people in the culture capital of the world because my day-to-day life was so different then. The journey was filled with bumps, and the dream became exhausting at times. But in the pursuit of the dream, my faith was refined and my identity was solidified.

Dreaming with God does that—it causes our faith to be formed and our identity to be galvanized. The challenges that come along the way are make-it-or-break-it types of events. But when you are living in intimate relationship with a loving God, you actually get strengthened by every challenge. Sometimes dreaming with God even creates contradictions in your current life and self-perception when there are gaps between where you are and where you are called to be. But these contradictions put you on a crash course for dynamic change and challenge you to reach out for more of Jesus so He can form you and your future.

To dream wild, you have to actually pursue this change and the tools that will catapult you forward. I wish I'd had this book twenty years ago, but I am glad to be holding it now. I have learned that I need tools to go after the faith lifestyle of a dreamer. Most of the time no one will fully dream your dreams with you except Christ in you. That means it's going to take the work of faith, the lifestyle of risk, and the biggest thing: learning to keep your heart open and healthy at all times. This book is filled with insights that will help you do just that.

Jennifer has created an incredible resource for you. I am literally using it now with my wife to believe for upgraded dreams and to shed off some old patterns and unbelief. I think this book works so well because Jennifer shares vulnerably about her life and what she experienced before her dreams were fulfilled. She touches on the theological points from a very personal perspective. She takes you on a discipleship journey that is in bite-size but very meaty pieces.

When applied, this tool will cause you to make different choices because you will be tying your whole value and identity to Jesus. You will release wrong thinking and bad beliefs or fears. You will allow yourself to dream with God, and I am convinced you will come out on the other end, standing in the middle of dreams fulfilled. The change will be so dramatic you won't even recognize your life, nor will longtime friends and family, because it will be more amazing than anything you could have built on your own.

—Shawn Bolz
Director, Bolz Ministries (www.bolzministries.com)
Author, *Translating God*, *God Secrets*,
and *Keys to Heaven's Economy*

THE WILD PROPHECY THAT RADICALLY CHANGED MY LIFE

ONE *LOGOS* WORD from God can shift your life—but one *rhema* word from His Spirit can radically revolutionize your existence. Put another way, the written Word of God—known in the Greek as *logos*—will renew your mind as you meditate on it day and night. But a *rhema* word of God—an utterance that proceeds out of His very mouth to your hungry heart—can open your eyes to realities you never thought possible.

I've prophesied over thousands of people and received my fair share of prophetic words over the years. But one wild prophecy I received in my worship closet intensely inspired my heart, challenged my mind, and compelled me to chase after the God of my dreams—the One who ultimately makes all our dreams come true.

One simple, yet profound, prophecy has changed and will continue to change my life. That inspired utterance is also changing the lives of people around the world—and it will change your life too if you will grab hold of what the Lord is saying and press past the soulish, fleshly, and demonic obstacles in the pathway to its manifestation. This is the prophetic word:

I am marking you with My glory. I am changing you from the inside out. It's time to embark on a new season of chasing Me. You will be more effective. You will be more efficient. You will do more with less. You can't see it. It's hard for you to believe it, but I am the author of it.

Take the limits off. Take the lid off. I am opening new doors for you. It's not just about favor. I'm shifting you from favor to open heavens. You will not strive, but you will not lack. I have gone before you to make a way for you. The divine connections are right around the corner. They are just ahead. You will see them and know them.

I am indeed giving you double for your trouble. I will put in your hands as much as you can believe Me for. How much can you believe Me for? Dream again. Dream big dreams. Dream wild dreams. Dream with Me, and I will dream with you.

I decided to take God up on His offer to dream. Supernatural, explosive breakthroughs are happening—and I know I haven't seen *anything* yet. *You* can grab hold of this word too! God is no respecter of persons (Rom. 2:11). There's nothing particularly special about me. I always say the best thing I have going for me is that I refused to give up. And believe me, I've had plenty of reasons to. I'm sure you have too.

FROM WILD TRAGEDY TO WILD DREAMS

When my husband abandoned me in 1999, leaving me in massive debt with our then-two-year-old baby, I shook my fist at an invisible God I did not yet know and demanded answers for the injustice. He was silent then, but I know now He was watching over me and protecting me. His thoughts toward me were thoughts of peace and not of evil, to give me a future and a hope (Jer. 29:11). He had wild dreams for me before I ever accepted His Son into my heart.

About eighteen months after my husband disappeared and left my life in utter shambles, I was arrested for a crime I didn't commit. I was facing five years in prison—a sentence that would have left my daughter essentially orphaned. Helpless and hopeless, I finally cried out to God—and He delivered me from the enemy's plot to destroy our lives. Wearing a bright orange jumpsuit in a dark county jail, I surrendered my heart to the One who created me, and the peace of God that passes all understanding guarded my heart and mind in Christ Jesus (Phil. 4:7).

It was in this setting—a county jail filled with prostitutes, drug addicts, thieves, and all manner of violent criminals—that I heard the still, small voice of God for the first time. In the face of impossibility God taught me that "all things are possible to him who believes" (Mark 9:23). He taught me to dream an impossible dream even when everyone around me thought I was foolish to hold out hope.

I'll always remember my first post-salvation experience with the Lord. The Holy Spirit showed me in the Word and spoke to my heart that I would be released from jail on the fortieth day after my arrest. Being a new convert, I had no idea the number forty was a symbol of testing and trial, but every time I opened my Bible, I read an account that revolved around that number: Moses's forty years in Egypt, the Israelites' forty years in the desert, Noah's experience with the forty-day flood, Jesus's forty days in the wilderness.

After several days of supernatural guidance through the Word, the Holy Spirit made it clear to my heart that I would be released from the injustice of imprisonment in forty days. It seemed impossible, considering the judge had refused to allow me bail three times—and this same judge was on vacation well after the fortieth day of my captivity, so it seemed there was no way I would be released on that day. All I could say was, "But God."

On the fortieth day of my incarceration, I was called into a holding cell with other inmates. I was never tried or convicted by my accusers. I never stood before an earthly judge. Thankfully *the* judge—Jesus Christ—is not a man that He should lie. I was released on the fortieth day, just as the Holy Spirit told me I would be. A judge ruled the whole case a "gross injustice." The accusations were washed away, sort of like my sins when I accepted Jesus.

God has restored my life in beautiful ways, more than making up for the injustice of being abandoned with a baby and falsely accused and imprisoned. I was eventually promoted to serve as senior editor of *Charisma* magazine, which is produced by one of the largest Christian media companies in the world. I have authored dozens of books, ministered in several nations, and appeared on many TV and radio broadcasts, and I direct a thriving revival center ministry in Fort Lauderdale, Florida. Most importantly I have a special relationship with my beautiful daughter, as we have weathered the storms of life together.

And this is just the beginning. The "dream wild" revelation promises the best is yet to come, that my latter shall be greater than my past (Hag. 2:9). All I have to do is come into agreement with it, be a doer of the prophetic word, keep my spiritual eyes wide open for those divine connections, and stretch my faith to see the impossible become possible in my life. I'm on a new journey with God to dream wild. God is inviting you on the same journey.

GOD'S DREAMS ARE BIGGER THAN YOUR DREAMS

Could it be possible that the reason you haven't seen some of your dreams come true is because you are dreaming too small? I believe so. Isaiah 55:9 gives us the Lord's perspective on the matter: "For as the heavens are higher than the earth, so are My ways higher than your ways, and My thoughts than your thoughts." It would also be true to say His dreams are wilder than our dreams.

See, when I was in jail those forty days, my dream was just to be free from the bars that bound me. I never dreamed I would preach the gospel in the nations of the earth. When I was set free from the county's captivity, my only dream was to write for Jesus. When I finally landed a freelance article in *Charisma* magazine, I thought I saw my dream come true in its fullness. I never imagined I would one day become the chief editor of the magazine or write best-selling Christian books. But God did. God's dream for me was wilder than my dream. God's dream for you is wilder than your dream.

When my husband left me, he also left behind massive amounts of debt—even IRS debt. My dream was to not get harassing phone calls from collectors during dinner. My dream was to one day have a strong enough credit score to purchase a home. I never dreamed that I would one day become completely debt-free and own four homes and twenty-three acres of land. But God did. God's dream for me was wilder than my dream. God's dream for you is wilder than your dream.

I always dreamed of making my own music CD. I wrote songs in the past that the church worship team would sing—but I can't sing! One day I was driving in the car with a friend of mine who had just put out a new CD, and he offered to produce one for me. That hit my spirit. I realized I can't sing, but there is one thing I can do—I can prophesy. I recorded a CD called *Dream Wild*, with prophetic words against music, that is firing people up. That was the beginning of my dreaming wild, and I don't plan to stop!

COOPERATING WITH THIS PROPHECY

When it comes to prophecy, I've learned that when the word of the Lord comes unto us—whether it's the still, small voice speaking to your heart or a word the Lord delivers through someone else—we need to cooperate with the grace of God to see a thing come to pass. In other words, personal prophecies are almost always conditional. God will do His part, but you have to do your part. The good news is God will give you His grace to do your part. With that in mind, let's line the "dream wild" prophecy up with Scripture, weighing it out, so we can put our faith on it and take action in the pages ahead.

The Lord says, "I am marking you with My glory."
In John 17:22 Jesus said: "I have given them the glory which You gave Me, that they may be one even as We are one." Ephesians 1:13 tells us we are marked in Christ with a seal to the praise of His glory. Christ in us is the hope of glory (Col. 1:27). He has created us for His glory (Isa. 43:7). You are "fearfully and wonderfully made" in His image (Ps. 139:14, NIV). Cooperate with this word by searching out deeper revelations of who you are in Christ and who He is in you.

The Lord says, "I am changing you from the inside out."
Second Corinthians 3:18 assures us: "But we all, seeing the glory of the Lord with unveiled faces, as in a mirror, are being transformed into the same image from glory to glory by the Spirit of the Lord." Paul offered these Spirit-inspired words: "I am confident of this very thing, that He who began a good work in you will perfect it until the day of Jesus Christ" (Phil. 1:6). The Word charges us in Romans 12:2: "Do not be conformed to this world, but be transformed by the renewing of your mind, that you may prove what is the good and acceptable and perfect will of God." Sometimes the reason we aren't seeing our wild dreams come to pass is because we're not yet ready to maintain the blessing God wants to pour out.

God is preparing our hearts to receive and steward the manifestation of our wild dreams. We need to surrender to this work.

The Lord says, "It's time to embark on a new season of chasing Me. You will be more effective. You will be more efficient. You will do more with less."

In Matthew 6:33 Jesus tells us, "But seek first the kingdom of God and His righteousness, and all these things shall be given to you." There are many, many scriptures relating to the mandate and promise of seeking God—too many to offer in full here. You can study these and others for yourself: Deuteronomy 4:29; Job 5:8–9; Psalm 32:10; Psalm 63:1; Psalm 119:10; Proverbs 8:17; Isaiah 55:6–7; Jeremiah 29:12–14; Lamentations 3:25; Matthew 7:7–8; Hebrews 11:6. Sometimes the reason we aren't seeing our dreams come true is because we are chasing our dreams instead of chasing the God who gave us the dreams. If we are not careful, we will make our dreams an idol. The Lord is clear: "You shall have no other gods before Me" (Exod. 20:3).

The Lord says, "You can't see it. It's hard for you to believe it, but I am the author of it."

We see in part, and we prophesy in part (1 Cor. 13:9). We see through a glass dimly (1 Cor. 13:12). Jesus is the author and finisher of our faith (Heb. 12:2). We don't have to know it all—we just have to be satisfied to know the One who does. Like the man in the Bible whose son was oppressed, we need to cry, "Lord, I believe. Help my unbelief!" (Mark 9:24).

The Lord says, "Take the limits off. Take the lid off."

God is a limitless God. There are no limitations in Him. He created the universe. He created you. We need to ask the Lord for a deeper revelation of His limitless power, His limitless grace, His limitless love, His limitless mercy, and so on. The only thing that can ultimately limit us is our thoughts. Proverbs 23:7 tells us we become what we think about ourselves. Limiting beliefs about ourselves or our God can hinder us from pursuing His wild dreams for us.

The Lord says, "I am opening new doors for you."

Speaking of Jesus, Isaiah 22:22 tells us: "The key of the house of David I will lay on his shoulder. Then he shall open, and no one shall shut. And he shall shut, and no one shall open." God can open doors no man on earth and no devil in hell can shut. Sometimes before He does that, He shuts doors that He doesn't want you to walk through—or doors you've already walked through. It's possible you're dreaming a dream that's not in God's dream for you. We need to ask the Lord for discernment so we can recognize the right doors and walk through them—and walk away from doors He is closing.

The Lord says, "It's not just about favor. I'm shifting you from favor to open heavens."

God covers us with favor as a shield (Ps. 5:12). John 1:16 says, "We have all received from His fullness grace upon grace." The Greek word translated *grace* in that verse also means favor.[1] Favor is good, but open heavens are better. Malachi 3:10 speaks of an open heaven, explaining: "Bring all the tithes into the storehouse, that there may be food in My house, and test Me now in this, says the LORD of Hosts, if I will not open for you the windows of heaven and pour out for you a blessing, that there will not be room enough to receive it." In Genesis 28:12–13 Jacob received revelation in an open heaven. We hear the Lord's voice more clearly in an open heaven (Matt. 3:16–17). We may encounter Jesus in a new way in an open heaven (Acts 7:54–55; 9:3–5). Anything is possible under an open heaven!

The Lord says, "You will not strive, but you will not lack."

God has not called us to lack. God has called us to owe no man anything but to love him (Rom. 13:8–10). The only thing we are supposed to strive for is entering the rest of God (Heb. 4:9–11). We need to press into revelation of Jehovah-Jireh, which means "The Lord will provide."[2]

The Lord says, "I have gone before you to make a way for you."

Deuteronomy 31:8 promises: "The LORD, He goes before you. He will be with you. He will not fail you nor forsake you. Do not fear, nor be dismayed." In Isaiah 45:2 the Lord promises, "I will go before you and make the crooked places straight; I will break in pieces the gates of bronze and shatter the bars of iron." God can and does make a way for even the wildest dreams He gives us to come true in due season.

The Lord says, "The divine connections are right around the corner. They are just ahead. You will see them and know them."

Ruth and Naomi had a divine connection (Ruth 1:16–17). Jonathan and David had a divine connection (1 Sam. 18:1). Paul and Barnabas had a divine connection (Acts 13:1–3). Paul and Timothy had a divine connection (1 Tim. 1:2). God will bring divine connections—and even divine reconnections—in your life as part of bringing your wild dreams to pass. We need to watch for them carefully.

The Lord says, "I am indeed giving you double for your trouble."

Job got double for his trouble (Job 42:10). Isaiah 61:7 promises, "Instead of your shame you shall have double honor, and instead of humiliation they shall rejoice over their portion. Therefore, in their land they shall possess a double portion; everlasting joy shall be theirs." And Zechariah 9:12 assures us, "Return to your stronghold, prisoners who now have hope. Today I declare that I will return to you a double portion."

Finally, the Lord says, "I will put in your hands as much as you can believe Me for. How much can you believe Me for? Dream again. Dream big dreams. Dream wild dreams. Dream with Me, and I will dream with you." That is an open invitation to stretch your faith, to move from mustard-seed faith to mountain-moving faith.

In the pages of this book you'll learn how to build your faith for your wild dreams and how to overcome obstacles and fight the good fight of faith for your heavenly aspirations. You will also find practical tools to help you dream wild with God.

Dream Wild is unlike most books. You can use this as a devotional, going through day by day to find inspiration on your journey—and this is what I recommend upon first read. Absorb the prophecies, the scriptures, the inspirational quotes, the raw stories, and the practical advice this book has to offer. Once you've read through the manuscript once, you'll find this is a field guide to living your dreams. It offers a sort of blueprint for seeing your dreams come true.

Although this book offers thirty days of teaching and inspiration, don't let the format pressure you. The chapters are short enough that you can read through one in as little as fifteen minutes day by day. But you may choose to dwell on a certain principle in any given chapter for weeks at a time, depending on where you find yourself in your heavenly exploits. Don't feel pressured to move through this too quickly. When the Holy Spirit illuminates something to your heart, take all the time you need to dwell on that truth so you can renew your mind and build your faith for the next stage of your spiritual expedition.

When you need some inspiration, for example, you can meditate on the dream wild prophecy that will inspire faith in your heart. When your past starts to haunt you, frustration creeps in, or some other obstacle arises in your soul, you can read selections from part 2 over and over again. When storms come raging against your wild dream, the chapters in part 3 will strengthen your heart. And when you are ready to run with the wild dream God put in your heart, go step by step through part 4, and you'll move closer and closer to realizing your heart's desires.

You'll find the exercises in each chapter thought-provoking and perhaps even confrontational at times. I'd recommend reading this book with a pen in hand and a journal by your side so you can pour out your heart to the Holy Spirit, write down what He tells you, strategize with Him, record your prayers, and more. When your dream comes true, your journal will serve as a precious memorial of your journey with the Lord toward His dream for your life.

Are you ready to dream? If so, let's begin.

Part One

DARE TO DREAM WILD

JESUS INVITES YOU TO DREAM WILD

*The Holy Spirit is saying, "Look at the impossible
and call it possible. Your circumstances will not
defy My will for your life. Your declarations
will defy the enemy's plans. Trust Me."*

I'D RATHER DREAM wild dreams and get half of what I am dreaming for than dream small dreams and get all of what I am dreaming for. Our heavenly Father gives us permission to dream wild and is able to bless us beyond our wildest dreams. Indeed, dreaming wild is not a new concept. Jesus invited us to dream wild over and over again in the Gospels.

Jesus said, "I will do whatever you ask in My name, that the Father may be glorified in the Son. If you ask anything in My name, I will do it" (John 14:13–14). That's a wild promise for those who dare to dream wild! That's an invitation to limitless dreaming. Oh, and in case you are wondering what the words *whatever* and *anything* mean in those verses, let these Greek definitions spark your faith.

Whatever in John 14:13 comes from the Greek word *an*. Although it has no English equivalent, according to Strong's concordance, it essentially means "whatever."[1] *Merriam-Webster* defines *whatever* as "anything or everything" and "no matter what."[2] That covers, well, everything in God's heart for you. The word *thing* in John 14:14 comes from the Greek word *tis*, which essentially means "certain (thing)."[3] It's a specific thing. We can dream with wild

13

specifics—and we should. We should pray wildly specific prayers so there's no second-guessing where the blessings come from.

Jesus said, "If you remain in Me, and My words remain in you, you will ask whatever you desire, and it shall be done for you" (John 15:7). You could put it another way: ask whatever you dream. The Greek word translated *desire* in that verse is *thelō*. According to the Outline of Biblical Usage it means "to will, have in mind, intend; to be resolved or determined, to purpose; to desire, to wish...to like to do a thing, be fond of doing; to take delight in, have pleasure."[4] God really will give you the desires of your heart when you delight in Him (Ps. 37:4). He really will.

Jesus said, "Truly, truly I say to you, whatever you ask the Father in My name, He will give it to you. Until now you have asked nothing in My name. Ask, and you will receive, that your joy may be full" (John 16:23–24). God wants you to receive everything Christ died to make possible for you. Remember the dream wild prophecy. The Lord said, "I will put in your hands as much as you can believe Me for. How much can you believe Me for?" Our heavenly Father is inviting us to dream impossible dreams that really aren't impossible—for Him.

WILD DREAMING WITH MARK 9:23 IN MIND

"If you can believe, all things are possible to him who believes" (Mark 9:23). In case you haven't caught the drift yet, when Jesus said "all things," He meant all things. The concept of "all things" runs throughout the entire Bible from cover to cover. In fact, the King James Version speaks of "all things" 201 times. But did Jesus really mean "all things are possible to him who believes"? And if so, what does "all things" really mean?

Of course, Jesus meant what He said. When God speaks, truth is established, and once that truth is established, nothing can change it. God does not have a loose tongue, and He doesn't make promises He can't keep. We may go back on our word, but God doesn't go back on His word. He is not a man that He should lie, nor the Son of Man that He should repent (Num. 23:19).

We need to settle this "all things" question in our hearts once and for all because sometimes you can't find a specific promise in Scripture to stand on. Oh, the scripture may be there, but you may be too overwhelmed to find it, or you may not have enough knowledge of the Word to know what belongs to you.

It has been said that a man who believes all things are possible approaches the unconventional with an open mind and a fearless heart. An open mind and a fearless heart set the stage for wild dreams to come true.

So then what does "all things" mean in Scripture? Well, I don't know about you, but I take God's Word literally. I don't try to figure out what He meant. He meant what He said. So when God says "all," He means "all." He doesn't mean some, much, or most. He means all. One dictionary definition of *all* is "as much as possible."⁵ So you might say, "As much as possible is possible if you believe." And we know that with God all things are possible (Matt. 19:26). With pure faith nothing will be impossible to you (Matt. 17:20).

Matthew 17:20 carries an important point: accessing all things possible requires faith. You have to develop faith to see wild dreams come to pass in your life. Just so there's no way for the devil to talk you out of the truth that's in the rest of this book, let's go ahead and dissect the word *all* once and for all and reinforce your faith for all things possible to him who believes (Mark 9:23). Begin building your faith for the manifestation of wild dreams now!

The New Testament word for all in scriptures that reference "all things" comes from the Greek word *pas*. Guess what it means? It's very clear. *Pas* means "all." So what does *all* mean? *All* means the "whole amount, quantity or extent of."⁶ *All things* means everything. Nothing is excluded in all things. All things includes all that exists. In fact, *all* means more than that—because if what you need doesn't already exist, the Creator of heaven and earth can make it for you.

Now let me balance that out. If you ask with the wrong motives, forget it. James warns, "You ask, and do not receive, because you ask amiss, that you may spend it on your passions" (James 4:3). If you are asking for a big dream house because you lust after the admiration of men, you are abusing this principle and are in danger of tapping into New Age secrets. Don't go there. When I'm talking about wild dreams, I'm talking about things in line with God's will. I am not endorsing the prosperity gospel, though I do believe in prosperity. I am not endorsing name-it-claim-it, blab-it-grab-it, watered-down and hyped-up gospels.

But all that controversy has, to some extent, robbed genuine believers of the determination to press in for God's wild dreams for their lives. People stop praying for their lost family members because they think the case is too hard for God. No—believe for a miracle! People give up the battle against cancer because of the doctor's report. No—believe for a miracle.

Sometimes people die in a lost condition. Sometimes people die from cancer. Sometimes you lose your house or your spouse. Despite the fact that no one has a smooth ride in every area of life all the time, we should still believe that God will work all things together for good to those who love Him and are called according to His purpose (Rom. 8:28). Indeed, there's a miracle in that verse! Sometimes we end up in impossible situations. That's why you need to build your faith for all things possible—for the God of wild dreams.

LEAVING BARRENNESS BEHIND

God is giving you permission to dream again, to dream big dreams—to dream wild dreams. Maybe you've experienced a season—or even a lifetime—of barrenness. You may relate to Abraham's story. His dream was to have an heir, but his wife was barren.

I looked up the Hebrew word for barren, and it simply means "barren." *Webster's Revised Unabridged Dictionary* defines *barren* as "unproductive; fruitless; unprofitable; empty; mentally dull; stupid."[7] The enemy wants to make you feel unproductive, fruitless, empty, mentally dull, and stupid, but God wants you to dream wild. Barrenness is not from the Lord. In Genesis 1:28 God charged us to be fruitful and multiply. The charge to be fruitful and multiply is not merely in the context of having children. God intends for us to be fruitful and multiply in the areas He is calling us to.

The Bible calls Abraham a friend of God (James 2:23). Abraham spoke to God like a friend in Genesis 15:2–6: "'Lord GOD, what will You give me, seeing I am childless and the heir of my house is Eliezer of Damascus?' Abram said, 'Since You have not given me any children, my heir is a servant born in my house.' Then the word of the LORD came to him, saying, 'This man will not be your heir, but a son that is from your own body will be your heir.' He brought him outside and said, 'Look up toward heaven and count the stars, if you are able to count them.' And He said to him, 'So will your descendants be.' Abram believed the LORD, and He credited it to him as righteousness."

Abram (later renamed Abraham) was ready to settle for less than God's wild dream for him. Maybe you have settled for less than God's best plan for your life. It's not too late to believe the Lord. It's never too late to dream again. I can only imagine Abraham counting the stars: "One, two, three, four, ten, twenty, one hundred, five hundred, one thousand—oops, I lost count. I have to start over." You can't count the stars. But Abraham chose to dream wild in the face of impossibilities. He chose to reach for the stars. Your life may look barren, your finances may look barren, your relationships may look barren, but your covenant with the God of all things possible gives you permission to dream wild!

Eleanor Roosevelt, an American politician, diplomat, and activist, and the longest-running first lady of the United States, is often quoted as saying, "The future belongs to those who believe in the beauty of their dreams."[8] Decide to believe your God, the dream giver.

DREAM WILD EXERCISE: MY DREAM IS DOABLE

The Lord wants you to dream wild. Accept His offer right now by meditating on Mark 9:23: "If you can believe, all things are possible to him who believes." Emphasize the words *all things*. Change out the words *all* and *possible* for some of their synonyms to drive the point home in your mind, renewing it with what the Word says:

> Each thing is possible.
> Every little thing is achievable.
> The whole shebang is feasible.
> The whole ball of wax is easy as pie.
> The greatest thing is realizable.
> The perfect thing is obtainable.
> The total thing is a breeze.
> The entire thing is probable.
> The complete thing is within reach.

DEVELOPING FAITH TO DREAM WILD

*The Holy Spirit is saying, "Don't let the devil lead
you and guide you. Let Me lead and guide you. The
devil will lead you into fear, worry, and overwhelm.
I will lead you into truth and abundant life. The
devil dreams of your distraction. I dream of your
destiny in Christ. Dream with Me. Follow Me."*

N OW FAITH IS the substance of things hoped for, the evidence
of things not seen" (Heb. 11:1). The Bible goes on to say that
by faith the elders obtained a good testimony (v. 2). Do you
want to build a good testimony? The first key to building faith to
dream wild is to understand that "the universe was framed by the
word of God, so that things that are seen were not made out of
things which are visible" (Heb. 11:3). God created all things out of
nothing by His spoken word—which again confirms that if something doesn't exist, He can make it for you.

The so-called Hall of Faith in Hebrews 11 calls out a number of
men and women whom the Holy Spirit offers up as examples of
wild dreamers. For example, by faith Noah built an ark to escape
the flood that wiped out almost every living thing on the earth.
People probably thought he was crazy for believing God, but he
saw his wild dream come true: divine protection. Settle this in
your heart now: oftentimes seeing your wild dream come to pass

means ignoring the scoffers and refusing to consider their arguments against your wonder-working faith. When man comes against you for daring to dream wild, remember that God, the ultimate dreamer, is on your side.

By faith Sarah received strength to conceive a child when she was barren. By faith Abraham was willing to sacrifice that same promised child. Now that's faith! Think about it for a minute. Abraham and Sarah had believed for a wild dream of having an heir for many, many years. Once the dream manifested—his name was Isaac—and grew into his teenage years, Abraham dared to dream God would raise him from the dead if he sacrificed him in obedience.

Sometimes God will ask you to make a wild sacrifice by faith to see if you really trust Him. When you are willing to lay your dream on the altar for His glory, He'll often provide a ram in the bush for you (Gen. 22:13). In other words, He's not trying to kill your dream—He just wants to make sure you won't put your dreams before Him if He helps you achieve the promise. And even if He allows you to make the sacrifice, He'll give you something far better in return—He will make your wildest dreams come true. God is not going to leave you hanging!

DEVELOPING WILD FAITH

Believing God for the wildest of wild dreams isn't always an easy road, but the only time it's impossible is without faith. The devil works to rob your faith and uses smoke and mirrors—people and circumstances—to do it. That's why you can't just seek God for what He can do for you. You have to seek Him for who He is. And you can't just seek Him when things are going good (or when things are going bad). You have to diligently seek Him.

Hebrews 11:6 says, "And without faith it is impossible to please God, for he who comes to God must believe that He exists and that He is a rewarder of those who diligently seek Him." At this point you believe in God and you believe He wants to bless you. That puts you in the realm of believing for wild dreams. But do you diligently seek Him? Or do you just seek Him when it's convenient for your busy schedule? Do you pencil God in and try to seek Him when you can, or are you diligently seeking Him? *Diligent* means steady, earnest, and energetic effort. Does that describe your

God seeking? Many times miracles are unexpected. But sometimes miracles demand what I call pursuing faith.

What is the pursuing kind of faith? Pursuing faith is faith that presses in like the woman with the issue of blood. She was plagued with a problem for twelve years and endured plenty of suffering from doctors. She spent all the money she had and got worse instead of better. Maybe you can relate. But then she heard about Jesus. "She had heard the reports concerning Jesus, and she came up behind Him in the throng and touched His garment, for she kept saying, If I only touch His garments, I shall be restored to health. And immediately her flow of blood was dried up at the source, and [suddenly] she felt in her body that she was healed of her [distressing] ailment" (Mark 5:27–29, AMPC).

The woman with the issue of blood pressed in to God to see her wild dream of healing manifest. Most likely she had to crawl on the ground through the crowd to reach the hem of His garment. She probably had to combat all manner of imaginations. She even broke the law by coming out of her house in this unclean state. She could have been stoned. But she had pursuing faith that focused on a single goal: receiving her wild dream.

GOD'S WORD IS OUR FOUNDATION

The first key to building faith to dream wild is to know what the Word says. It sounds simple, but it's the genesis of the supernatural. God's Word is the foundation upon which we build our faith. If we build our faith in Christ, who is the Word, then we won't be washed up when the rains of trouble come pouring down, or when a flood of trials comes crashing against our souls, or when the winds of tribulation come beating against our lives. Put another way, when we know what God's Word says on any given topic, we can work with the Holy Spirit to renew our minds with that truth so when the enemy comes whispering his lies, we'll flat-out reject them before they can take root in our souls.

The soul is a gateway to your spirit man. You hear the Word with your natural ears and read it with your natural eyes. When your soul prospers with the Word of God, it causes prosperity in other areas of your life. John called out two aspects of prosperity that faith in the Word brings: "Beloved, I pray that all may go well with you and that you may be in good health, even as your soul is well" (3 John 1:2). When your soul prospers with the Word of God, all dreams become possible.

Even if you're a bit jaded because you've waited and watched others realize their wild dreams while you are doing everything you can to get God's attention, I'm here to tell you that your time is coming. It's possible to build faith for the wildest dreams. It's possible to build your faith to receive the miraculous! Faith comes by hearing and hearing and hearing and hearing the Word (Rom. 10:17). So listen up, meditate on the truth you read in this chapter, and prepare your heart to see miracles—all things possible—in your life.

Take Baby Steps Toward Your Wild Dreams

In Matthew 18 Jesus talked about childlike faith, but I want to introduce the concept of baby steps. Whether you are a brand-new believer or a seasoned veteran who's met with disappointments over unfulfilled promises—or somewhere in between—taking baby steps is a strategic approach to building faith to dream wild.

In other words, work your way up to wonder-working faith. Believe God for what your soul tells you is possible before you believe Him for what your soul tells you is impossible. With a few easy wins under your belt, you can tell your soul to shut up when it rises up in disbelief at the wild dream you are believing God for. You can remind yourself of the string of prayer answers you've received and build your faith in the goodness of God before you release your faith to see your dreams come true.

With this "baby steps" concept in mind, let's do a quick review of some of Jesus's words while He walked the earth. First, He promised us that with God all things are possible (Matt. 19:26). Soon thereafter He assured us that whatever we ask in prayer, if we believe, we will receive (Matt. 21:22). He also guaranteed all things are possible to him who believes (Mark 9:23).

These are great and precious promises that must not be minimized. Jesus wasn't making promises just so He could take up a big offering at the end of the message. Jesus cannot lie. He is the Truth. When He says something, you can believe it. Jesus said all things are possible. The only catch: we have to believe it.

That said, don't start off trying to believe for the whole shebang at once. If your life is a mess, if you've been walking in doubt and unbelief for years, stretch your faith to receive something small before you charge after your wild dream so the enemy can't so easily shipwreck your faith with a little rainstorm. Much like physical strength is built up by first lifting light weights and later lifting heavier weights, faith is built up by believing God first for smaller things and later for bigger things.

Now, I'm not saying you can't charge out there and believe God right now for the dream of all dreams. I'm just suggesting that if you've struggled to receive in the past, wisdom may dictate nurturing your faith by feeding it smaller victories until it becomes strong enough to overcome the world. You can do all things through Christ who strengthens you (Phil. 4:13).

FAITH IS YOUR BASELINE

One of faith's prerequisites is believing that God can do it. We know that God is all-powerful and all-knowing. He can do anything. Nothing is too hard for Him (Jer. 32:17). He is merciful and gracious, full of wisdom and might. God is able to do exceedingly, abundantly above all that we ask or think, according to the power that works within us (Eph. 3:20). He is the all-sufficient One. He is the Creator of all things. And remember: if something doesn't exist, He can make it for you.

You may not have a hard time believing that God can do anything. But you may have a problem believing He wants to do it for you. Keep this in mind: Romans 8:32 says, "He who did not spare His own Son, but delivered Him up for us all, how shall He not with Him also freely give us all things?"

Think about that for a minute. God delivered up Jesus for you. He already made the ultimate sacrifice for you. He was separated from His Son. He experienced the pain of that separation—and He did it willingly. And if that's not enough, once you receive Jesus by faith, He's willing to give you all things possible by faith. What a God we serve! God is not holding back from dreaming wild. That should cause thankfulness to rise up in your heart.

As Mary McLeod Bethune once said, "Without faith, nothing is possible. With it, nothing is impossible."[1]

DREAM WILD EXERCISE:
BUILDING FAITH FOR THE MIRACULOUS

Building miraculous faith starts with a decision and requires determination. Sometimes wild dreams fall into your lap, but most of the time they require pursuing faith. Take some time to consider which of God's promises have eluded you. Now decide in your heart in this moment that you will do whatever it takes to see God's best—even miraculous dreams—manifest in your life. But don't stop there. Put some action behind your decision. Pick up your Bible, and find the scriptures to build your faith for the impossible. Write them down, and keep them in front of your eyes every day. Post them on your refrigerator. Put a copy in your car or your purse. Start now!

UNLOCKING YOUR WILD DREAMS WITH HOLY SPIRIT'S HELP

The Holy Spirit is saying, "Dreaming is not an option. Your imagination is always working. You're always dreaming. It's a matter of whether you're going to dream the dreams I have put in your heart or the dreams the enemy has put in your soul. Your dream life is up to you. Cast down the enemy's dreams, and dream with Me."

W HEN I WAS on a mission trip one summer, a wise man called me over out of the blue and read 1 Corinthians 14:2 to me: "For he who speaks…" I wasn't expecting it, but I knew I needed to heed what he was saying. I knew I needed to begin praying in the Spirit much more.

How do miraculous dreams come to pass at the perfect time? It's a mystery, really. No one can explain how blind eyes can suddenly see or how deaf ears can suddenly hear or how cancer suddenly disappears or how limbs suddenly grow back—or even how someone gets born again, gets delivered from depression, loses the taste for drugs, and experiences other miracles. In much the same way, the dynamics of miraculous dreams coming true are a mystery. We can pray, believe, and take action, but God's ways are higher than our ways.

When you speak in unknown tongues, you are speaking mysteries to God. Could it be possible that some of those mysteries are unlocking wild dreams? I believe so. When that wise man read 1 Corinthians 14:2 to me on the mission field, he was giving me a key to unlocking God's dreams in my life. I left that encounter praying in the Spirit as much as I possibly could. I prayed and prayed and prayed some more. And I began to see wisdom and revelation open up to me. I began to see miracles taking place in my life—doors opening that no man could have opened. It didn't all happen at once. I've diligently prayed in the Spirit—more in some seasons than in others—for years. And I am convinced this has unlocked God's destiny for me.

Paul put it this way in 1 Corinthians 2:9–12:

> But as it is written, "Eye has not seen, nor ear heard, nor has it entered into the heart of man the things which God has prepared for those who love Him." But God has revealed them to us by His Spirit. For the Spirit searches all things, yes, the deep things of God. For what man knows the things of a man, except the spirit of man which is in him? Likewise, no one knows the things of God, except the Spirit of God. Now we have received not the spirit of the world, but the Spirit which is of God, so that we might know the things that are freely given to us by God.

MISTAKING MIRACLES FOR SHEER COINCIDENCE

I've seen supernatural debt cancellation. I've seen God intervene in life-and-death situations. I've seen God position me in places only He could and, again, open doors no man could open. Sometimes what looks like a coincidence is a miracle. Remember, the definition of *miracle* is "an extraordinary event manifesting divine intervention in human affairs."[1]

Here's a little miracle testimony for you: I once received an email from the producers of Sid Roth's *It's Supernatural!* television program. The producer wanted to explore the possibility of having me on a weeklong radio series and then a television broadcast. They ordered several of my books and CDs to review and particularly appreciated one work called *Faith Magnified*. Within weeks I was flying up to Charlotte, North Carolina, to tape a radio broadcast that goes to many nations in the world. I was also collecting large checks from the sale of the books and CDs.

Ironically, I had a brand-new book coming out in two months, *The Spiritual Warrior's Guide to Defeating Jezebel*. I figured my publicist had reached out to Sid Roth's ministry to pitch an appearance. But I was wrong. When I saw that the late Brownsville revivalist Steve Hill, who imparted much wisdom to me, had been on the show a few weeks earlier, I figured he had recommended me. But when I emailed Steve, he said he had not mentioned my name to Sid Roth.

Next, I reasoned that it was my exposure through *Charisma* magazine that turned their heads. But I was confused that they chose the *Faith Magnified* book because I am known more widely for my teachings on prophetic ministry and spiritual warfare than for those on faith. In fact, I've written several books on faith despite folks telling me that Kenneth Hagin already said everything there was to say about faith and that faith books don't sell. I wrote faith books despite the naysayers because God put it on my heart to write them. In other words, I wasn't doing it for the money; I was doing it out of obedience.

I finally asked one of the producers how they decided to reach out to me, and she said she didn't know. But when I was in Charlotte, the truth came out: One of the assistants decided to do a Google search for "Jennifer" and "ministry." Wouldn't you know it, the first result on the Google results was my website. And wouldn't you know it, they didn't pick up on my prophetic or warfare books. They picked up on the faith materials that God put on my heart to write despite the naysayers. And I was richly blessed financially because of it. I call that a miracle.

Similarly, I landed my position as an editor of *Charisma* magazine through what looked like a coincidence. I received a stray email from one of the other editors there. I had written on a freelance basis for the magazine for many years, but it was nothing consistent, and I didn't know this particular editor. I wrote back, "???" The editor admitted he had written to me by mistake as he was gathering the email addresses of freelancers. The current news editor was moving into a new role, and the position was open. He asked me if I was interested.

Of course I was interested. But I was not willing to relocate. I had just bought a condo, and I was finally debt-free. This editor told me it was unlikely that they would hire me to work remotely for such a key position. Long story short, I prayed, and God opened that door. My wild dream came true. Coincidence? No. It was a miracle, and I believe ultimately it started with my speaking mysteries to God. It was also God's will. It wasn't me breaking down a door. It was God's plan. I had prayed it out in other tongues with the help of the Holy Spirit—speaking mysteries to God for years before my wild dream manifested.

WHEN YOU DON'T KNOW HOW TO PRAY

Have you ever felt as if you just don't know how to pray? You need to see something break open so you can take another step toward your God-given dreams, but you don't even know what to ask for other than, "God, give me a breakthrough!" There's nothing wrong with that prayer, but you might get your breakthrough faster if you pray in tongues.

Romans 8:26–27 informs, "Likewise, the Spirit helps us in our weaknesses, for we do not know what to pray for as we ought, but the Spirit Himself intercedes for us with groanings too deep for words. He who searches the hearts knows what the mind of the Spirit is, because He intercedes for the saints according to the will of God."

When your faith is at its weakest point, I recommend praying in the Spirit. If you can muster up enough faith to pray in the Spirit over a matter, the Holy Spirit will partner with you to raise supplications to the Father. We have to do our part—pray in tongues by faith—and He will do His part. Christ is interceding for us in heaven, and the Holy Spirit is praying with us on the earth. Why wouldn't we expect our God-given dreams to come true in His perfect timing?

In *Matthew Henry's Commentary on the Bible* the man of God wrote, "The Spirit, as an enlightening Spirit, teaches us what to pray for, as a sanctifying Spirit works and excites praying graces, as a comforting Spirit silences our fears, and helps us over all our discouragements. The Holy Spirit is the spring of all our desires and breathings towards God."[2]

Praying in the Spirit is praying a perfect prayer to a perfect God. When you pray in the Spirit, you are praying a perfect prayer, and you can expect a perfect answer. Your mind is unfruitful (1 Cor. 14:14), but that doesn't matter because it's not your mind that produces the miracle. It is the Spirit of God.

RECEIVING THE HOLY SPIRIT

How can you receive the Holy Spirit? You first have to believe the Holy Spirit is a gift from God. So let's look at what Jesus said as recorded in John 16:7: "Nevertheless I tell you the truth: It is expedient for you that I go away. For if I do not go away, the Counselor will not come to you. But if I go, I will send Him to you."

Did Jesus ever tell a lie? Of course not. Is He waiting for you to manifest perfect behavior before you can be filled with the Holy Spirit? Absolutely not! He wants to fill you with the Holy Spirit so you can be perfected, not because you already are. When you got saved, God didn't expect you to come to His throne all cleaned up to ask forgiveness. He knew you were a mess. He wanted you to come to His throne to find mercy and receive grace to clean up your mess. Now He wants to fill you with His Spirit so you can walk in His grace, which offers power to overcome any sinful habit.

Jesus said, "If you then, being evil, know how to give good gifts to your children, how much more will your heavenly Father give the Holy Spirit to those who ask Him?" (Luke 11:13). If you want to become white hot with passion for the Lord, if you need a spark, if you need to rekindle that love, ask the Lord to fill you to overflowing with His Holy Spirit. Why not pray right now before you move on through the pages of this book?

Pray with me:

> *Father God, I come to You in the name of Jesus. I thank You that You sent Your only begotten Son to save me, and I thank You that You desire to fill me with Your Holy Spirit. Jesus said, "How much more will your heavenly Father give the Holy Spirit to those who ask Him?" (Luke 11:13).*
>
> *Right now I ask You in the name of Jesus to fill me with Your Holy Spirit. I receive the indwelling of Your Spirit right now, and I confess by faith that I am Spirit-filled. I thank You that You have given me a prayer*

language to communicate with You, and I yield my tongue to Your Spirit right now. I expect to speak in tongues as the Spirit gives me utterance. I thank You and praise You. Amen!

When you pray in tongues, you are doing double duty. Not only are you praying the perfect prayer, thanks to the Helper; you are also building yourself up. Paul and Jude agreed on this. Paul wrote, "He who speaks in a tongue edifies himself" (1 Cor. 14:4). And Jude wrote, "But you, beloved, build yourselves up in your most holy faith. Pray in the Holy Spirit" (Jude 1:20).

As Johann Wolfgang von Goethe, a German writer and statesman, once said, "Dream no small dreams for they have no power to move the hearts of men."[3]

DREAM WILD EXERCISE: GET TO KNOW YOUR HELPER

Do you really know who the Holy Spirit is in your life? Take some time right now to think about who He is. He is your Helper. He will help you turn your dreams into reality. Get out your Bible, and do a study if you aren't familiar with the role He plays in your life. The Holy Spirit is always with you. Begin to interact with Him on a daily basis, and you will see your spiritual life change. You will grow. He will speak to you and give you revelation. He may be waiting on you to start the conversation.

RELEASING GOD'S WORD OVER YOUR WILD DREAMS

The Holy Spirit is saying, "What do you see? What do you really see? Look at what I am showing you. Meditate on the dreams I have put in your heart. Don't look at what the enemy tries to throw in your face. Focus on what I am showing you, and his fearful imaginations will not find a place in your soul and pollute your faith. Dream wild."

STILL HAVE MY list of confessions. I've had to print it out more than once over the years because it gets tattered after a while. But these Word-based confessions—when released in pure faith in the power of God—have supernaturally helped me see so-called impossible dreams come to pass in my life over and over again.

I believe wholeheartedly that it's the combination of praying in the Spirit, as I wrote about previously, and confessing the Word that has made all the difference. Praying in tongues or confessing the Word are powerful on their own, but combining the two super-charges your faith to dream wild.

Although I didn't realize it at the time, I discovered the power of confessing all things possible while I was in jail. If you've heard my story, which I share in my books *The Spiritual Warfare Battle Plan* and *Mornings With the Holy Spirit*, when I received a *rhema* word from God through Scripture that I would be released on the fortieth day, I began telling anyone who would listen. I began confessing the will of God over my life even in the face of an impossible situation.

I put my faith on that *rhema* word and confessed it as much as I could. And that word came to pass in short order. I was indeed released from jail on the fortieth day despite the natural circumstances that painted an impossible picture. It was a miracle! Of course God's wild dreams for your life don't always come to pass in forty days. Sometimes they come to pass much faster. And sometimes we need more patience mixed with our faith to inherit the promises of God (Heb. 6:12). Just don't stop confessing God's Word.

WHAT ARE YOU CONFESSING?

I've seen many seemingly impossible wild dreams on my confession list come to pass over the years. In my experience two keys are to make consistent confessions based on God's revealed will and to take action, because faith without works is dead. With that said, it's important to note that my faith for "all things possible" undergirded some of my confessions, which were merely desires of my heart rather than the revealed will of God. Let me give you a few examples.

Wild Dream Confession #1: "I am debt-free."

I was anything but debt-free when I began confessing this, but I believed it was the will of God because Romans 13:8 says, "Owe no one anything, except to love one another, for he who loves another has fulfilled the law." God doesn't want us in debt because the borrower is slave to the lender (Prov. 22:7). God has given us the power to create wealth (Deut. 8:18). And God wants us to prosper and be in health even as our soul prospers (3 John 1:2). So I confessed I was debt-free even though I had debt upon debt. Today I am debt-free.

Wild Dream Confession #2: "My taxes are settled, and taxes are not a burden to me."

When my husband left, I faced a large tax bill, and the IRS was coming after me for it. After the trauma of my husband's leaving, the false accusation that landed me in jail, and the life and business rebuilding I went through, I fell behind on my taxes. I had a large tax debt and was getting some pretty nasty letters from the government. Today my taxes are settled and taxes are not a burden to me.

Wild Dream Confession #3: "I own an oceanfront condo, and it is paid for."

When I began confessing that, it was purely a desire of my heart. I didn't have a word from God to stand on other than Psalm 37:4–5, "Delight yourself also in the LORD, and He shall give you the desires of your heart. Commit your way to the LORD, trust also in Him, and He shall bring it to pass" (NKJV). Today I not only own a condo that overlooks the ocean with no debt—I paid cash for it—I also own a second condo in North Miami Beach that's paid for and rented out. And I own two other homes and many acres of land.

Abraham's Wild, Dreamy Faith

I could go on and on, but I think you get the point. This is not a name-it-claim-it, blab-it-grab-it practice. This is not some new age philosophy or the so-called law of attraction. This is me acting like my Father. If Abraham can do it, why can't you? Consider what Paul wrote about the wild dreamer Abraham in Romans 4:16–22:

> Therefore the promise comes through faith, so that it might be by grace, that the promise would be certain to all the descendants, not only to those who are of the law, but also to those who are of the faith of Abraham, who is the father of us all (as it is written, "I have made you a father of many nations") before God whom he believed, and who raises the dead, and calls those things that do not exist as though they did.
>
> Against all hope, he believed in hope, that he might become the father of many nations according to what was spoken, "So shall your descendants be." And not being weak in faith, he did not consider his own body to be dead (when he was about a hundred years old), nor yet the deadness of Sarah's womb. He did not waver at the promise of God through unbelief, but was strong in faith, giving glory to God, and being fully persuaded that what God had promised, He was able to perform. Therefore "it was credited to him as righteousness."

The kind of faith that brings wild dreams into existence is faith that speaks of nonexistent things that God has foretold and promised as if they already existed (Rom. 4:17, AMPC). Indeed, the faith that brings the impossible dreams into existence is faith that does not grow weak when you look at your natural circumstances. The kind of faith that brings the miracle dreams into existence is faith that doesn't succumb to doubt or unbelief concerning the promise of God. The kind of faith that brings the impossible into existence is faith that gives praise and glory to God before the breakthrough because it believes God is able and mighty to keep His promises. The kind of faith that brings the desperate desires into existence is faith that understands God created all things—and if something doesn't exist, He can make it for you.

One more thing: When we confess the Word of God, we're supposed to confess it in faith. There was a time when I was confessing, confessing, and confessing some more when it dawned on me that it would be a waste of time if I wasn't in faith. So I asked the Holy Spirit, "How do I know that I'm in faith?" He answered me quickly: "The very fact that you're confessing the Word demonstrates that you have faith it will work! If you didn't believe the Word, you wouldn't take the time to confess it all day long!"

Do you get it? It's an act of our faith to confess the Word of God. Then, as we confess the Word of God, faith comes because we hear it. God makes it as easy as He can for us to believe. He even gave us the measure of faith to start off with (Rom. 12:3).

THE GOD WHO DREAMED AND CREATED ALL THINGS

God's Word contains creative power. If you are a born-again believer, you probably don't need to be convinced that God created all things. You already know that God created the heavens and the earth. You are sure God created man in His image. You are confident that God created all things through Jesus Christ. I want you to be more convinced, more sure, and more confident because it's a vital foundational concept to believe all things are possible to him who believes (Mark 9:23). It's vital to seeing your wild dreams come true!

If you are going to receive the impossible from God, you need to know He had you in mind when He created all things. You need to know it's His will for you to enjoy all the things He created. And you need to know that "all things" are unlimited. He won't run out before your faith grows enough to receive them. You don't have to be jealous when your neighbor gets the miracle you are believing for. If He's ever done it for anyone, He'll do it for you. And even if He hasn't ever done it for anyone, it's possible for you if you only believe. So let's start building our faith now by reviewing all the things God created.

John 1:1–3 tells us, "In the beginning was the Word, and the Word was with God, and the Word was God. He was in the beginning with God. All things were created through Him, and without Him nothing was created that was created."

Inspired by the Holy Spirit, John chose the words "all things." But he didn't stop there. Just in case anybody might misunderstand, he added a clause to the end of that statement. He said nothing—not one thing—came into being without Jesus. That's pretty emphatic—and it's absolutely true.

The apostle Paul put it this way: "To me, the very least of all saints, this grace was given, to preach to the Gentiles the incomprehensible riches of Christ, and to reveal for all people what is the fellowship of the mystery, which from the beginning of the ages has been hidden in God, who created all things through Jesus Christ" (Eph. 3:8–9).

The Book of Genesis outlines God's early creations (Gen. 1:1–26). We discover that God created everything with His word. He created light. He created vegetation. He created the sun, the moon, and the stars. He created the fish of the sea and every sort of animal. And He created man. He did it all with His word. This same creative power is within us—if we can believe that all things are possible. Nehemiah had this revelation:

> You alone are the Lord. You have made heaven, the heaven of heavens, with all their host, the earth and all that is on it, the seas and all that is in them; and You preserve them all. And the host of heaven worships You.
> —Nehemiah 9:6

Nehemiah takes it to the next level. He understood that not only did God create it all—God also preserves it all. That's an important, faith-building revelation. When we receive salvation, we receive so much more than our eternal security. We also receive all things pertaining to life and godliness. That means healing belongs to us, deliverance belongs to us, preservation belongs to us. In fact, the Greek word for salvation—*sozo*—implies the ideas of deliverance, safety, preservation, healing, and soundness.[1] That's the full gospel.

Solomon knew "the LORD has made all things for Himself, yes, even the wicked for the day of evil" (Prov. 16:4). Paul told a council at Athens that "God who made the world and all things in it, being Lord of heaven and earth, does not live in temples made by hands. Nor is He served by men's hands, as though He needed anything, since He gives all men life and breath and all things" (Acts 17:24–25).

Understanding that God created all things, gave life to all things, and preserves all things is part of your foundation for believing your wild dreams will come to pass.

To quote Thomas Edward Lawrence—a British archaeologist, military officer, diplomat, and writer in the early 1900s—"All men dream: but not equally. Those who dream by night in the dusty recesses of their minds wake in the day to find that it was vanity: but the dreamers of the day are dangerous men, for they may act their dreams with open eyes, to make it possible."[2]

DREAM WILD EXERCISE: LISTEN TO YOUR SELF-TALK

Have you ever really heard yourself speak? You could be talking yourself out of your miracle—literally! The words you speak are containers of power. The thoughts you vocalize carry the power of death and life (Prov. 18:21). Sometimes we develop poor speech habits. We speak out what we see instead of what the Word says. We speak out the doubt the enemy plants in our souls instead of what Scripture echoes in our spirits. Start thinking about what you talk about. Repent of speech that is contrary to God's wonder-working power. And then get your mouth in line with the Word of God.

DAY 5

DRAWING INSPIRATION FROM WILD DREAMERS

*The Holy Spirit is saying, "Your God-given dreams
can come true, but you have to pursue the God who
gave you the dreams. You also have to take Spirit-led
action in faith toward your godly goals. Yes, you'll meet
with spiritual warfare and natural stumbling blocks
and be tempted to give up. But don't give up! Don't
give in. If you seek first the kingdom of God and My
will for your life, you will see your dreams manifest in
Father's timing. Just keep pressing in! I am with you!"*

WHEN I WAS just six years old, I dreamed of going into outer space on a rocket. I drew rocket ships. I talked with my friends about outer space and what life would be like in the year 2000. In first grade I was convinced we'd all be racing around the world in Jetsons-style flying objects.

Growing up in Central Florida, I had easy access to Disney World. Epcot attractions fed my imagination with Walt Disney's view of what the future would hold. Way back in 1982, before Bill Gates and Steve Jobs became technology icons, Disney showed us a world where computers were in every home. A forward-thinking Disney even displayed touchscreen technology that has become popular only in recent years. Meanwhile, Future World forwarded the idea of e-commerce long before the advent of Amazon.com, as well as voice-recognition software demonstrated in a friendly robot called SMRT-1. Disney had wild dreams and a wild imagination. He truly saw into the future to where we are today.

Despite his innovation, Disney wasn't the first man to build a theme park. There were fairs in the Middle Ages, the world's fair was born in 1851, and mechanical rides emerged in the 1860s.[1] Sea Lion Park at Coney Island, the first enclosed theme park, opened in 1895.[2] For its part, Disneyland opened in California in 1955 with the moniker the "Happiest Place on Earth." Although his July 17 opening goes down in entertainment history as "Black Sunday" because rides broke down and the park did not have enough food and water on hand for eager visitors, Disney kept on dreaming wild and eventually opened the Magic Kingdom in Florida in 1971.[3]

Black Sunday didn't deter Disney because he had learned that holding on to wild dreams in the face of wild challenges will bring wild results. The challenges with building a mega theme park didn't stop him because he didn't have any stop in him. Disney had faced wild adversity and overcome disaster before, specifically with the making of *Snow White and the Seven Dwarfs*, the first feature-length animated film the world had ever seen—and one many still watch today.

THE WILD DREAM THAT CHANGED MOVIE-MAKING HISTORY

Walt Disney may be the ultimate dreamer. He said things such as: "All our dreams can come true, if we have the courage to pursue them." He quipped: "It's kind of fun to do the impossible." He declared: "If you can dream it, you can do it."[4] He advised: "First, think. Second, believe. Third, dream. And finally, dare."[5] You may think, "That's easy for him to say," but it wasn't.

Disney started making animated features in the 1920s. He found some success with the launch of Oswald the Lucky Rabbit under the Universal Studios banner. As the story goes, Disney lost Oswald but went on to create Mickey Mouse.[6] Disney created a series around the now-famous mouse but soon decided to chase a wilder dream—an idea that had been on his heart since he was a teenager. Disney set out to create the first full-length animated feature in the world: *Snow White and the Seven Dwarfs*.

In 1934 Disney gathered his staff and acted out the entire movie, even the role of the evil queen, then announced his grand vision to tell the story with cartoons. No one had ever attempted such a thing. His staff was reportedly excited—but most of Hollywood doubted Disney from the get-go. In fact, many referred to the attempt to create an eighty-minute animated film as "Disney's folly." Even his own wife warned him moviegoers would not sit through a cartoon fantasy about a young girl and a group of dwarfs. His flesh-and-blood brother believed it would be his undoing.[7] Hollywood was sure it would bankrupt the dreamer.

"It was prophesied that nobody would sit through such [a] thing," Disney said, "but there was only one way we could do it successfully and that was to plunge ahead and go for broke—shoot the works. There could be no compromising on money, talent or time...and this was at a time when the whole country was in the midst of a crippling depression."[8]

Maybe the enemy is prophesying against your wild dreams. Maybe you are surrounded by Debbie Doubters and Negative Nancys—even amid your own household. Maybe you don't have the support you need to do what you feel God is calling you to do. If so, you can make one of two choices: you can let the naysayers put out your fire, or you can let the skepticism fuel your determination to dream even wilder. Disney did the latter.

GO FOR BROKE

Indeed, Disney went for broke. He set out to do the impossible at a time when the Great Depression was raging. He estimated the film would cost between $250,000 and $500,000. "We had a little money coming in," Walt said, "but not enough to finance such a big deal. Our assets were pretty impressive, though—we had our studio and a backlog of marketable pictures—so we could get credit backing."[9]

Disney was going where no man had gone before—before *Star Trek* made the line popular. He was working with new technologies, such as a multiplane camera. He invested in synchronized sound and optical printers—and he trained his staff how to master these innovations.

"I had brought in specialists to help with our composition and our use of color, but we still had a fight on our hands for better animation," Disney told his daughter Diane, whose account was published in a 1956 edition of the *Saturday Evening Post*. "The kind of animation we were after was entirely new. Before that, it had been done by stunts: limber legs moving in trick runs like egg beaters. But in *Snow White* we wanted our action believable. We were after drama and pathos as well as laughter. You can't pull a tear from an audience with legs whirling like windmills."[10]

Pressure mounted on Disney's dreams as challenge after challenge plagued the production and the release date edged ever closer. Somehow Disney defied his skeptics and pulled off the impossible dream. *Snow White* premiered in Hollywood on December 21, 1937, at the Carthay Circle Theatre. Movie stars from the Golden Age of Hollywood were present, including Shirley Temple, Cary Grant, Ginger Rogers, George Burns, and Charlie Chaplin.[11] There wasn't a dry eye in the house. When Snow White died, Hollywood's elite stained the red velvet chairs of the famed theater with their tears.

Ultimately Disney spent $1.7 million on a cartoon in an era in which people were jobless, homeless, and foodless—but the film grossed $8 million, the most any film earned in its day.[12] Disney inspired the masses with a movie that goes down in history as a dream come true. Chaplin told the *Los Angeles Times* the film "even surpassed our high expectations. In Dwarf Dopey, Disney has created one of the greatest comedians of all time."[13] Disney won an honorary Academy Award for the movie, and several of the songs in the film earned Oscar nominations.[14] The movie was one of Adolf Hitler's personal favorites.[15]

DRAW INSPIRATION FROM WILD DREAMERS

We can—and should—draw inspiration from the Holy Spirit. But we can also draw inspiration from true stories of wild dreamers. There's Mackenzie Clare, the teenager who dreamed of being a model before an accident at age ten left her paralyzed. Clare never gave up on her dream. When she was on a prom date some years later, a photographer noticed Clare and enlisted her for a photo shoot she was planning.[16]

You may have heard of Terry Fox, one of Canada's most famous athletes. In 1977 Fox lost his right leg to cancer and determined in his heart to make a difference with the rest of his life. Three years later he launched Marathon of Hope, a campaign to raise money for cancer. He ran an average of twenty-six miles every day and raised awareness for cancer, inspiring a nation.[17] Then there's Ida Keeling, who set a record for the one-hundred-meter dash at the USA Track and Field Eastern Regional Open Championships at age ninety-seven.[18] She started running at age sixty-seven after a series of life tragedies and ran straight into her dream thirty years later.[19]

Pursuing your wild dreams is like running a race, and the Bible gives us plenty of encouragement along those lines. Paul tells us to run the race so we may obtain the prize (1 Cor. 9:24). Hebrews 12:1 admonishes us to lay aside every weight and sin and run our race with endurance. Paul also warns us not to run aimlessly (1 Cor. 9:26). There are many stories of wild dreamers such as Disney, Clare, Fox, and Keeling who can inspire you to stay focused on the finish line, where your wild dreams come true.

Start pursuing your wild dreams today. As the saying goes, there's no time like the present. To quote American self-help author Napoleon Hill, "Do not wait. The time will never be 'just right.'"[20]

DREAM WILD EXERCISE:
FIND INSPIRATION IN TESTIMONIES

Spend some time reading the stories of overcomers. You can easily find them online by typing in search terms such as "stories of dreams come true" or "inspiring stories of faith." Let the successes of people who have struggled to see their dreams come true fuel your faith to believe it can happen to you. Remember, God is no respecter of persons (Acts 10:34). Even if you can't find anyone who has a dream similar to yours, be encouraged by those who persevered past difficulties that may be even greater than yours to experience the sweet taste of manifested dreams.

Part Two

DEFEATING DREAM ENEMIES

DAY 6

TAKING THE LID OFF

The Holy Spirit is saying, "Think about what you want
out of life. Think about what you want in your family.
Think about what you want in your career. Think about
what you want in your health. Most importantly think
about what you want in your relationship with Me. Now
realize this: I am able to do more than you can ask, think,
or imagine. Dream big, take the limits off, and petition
heaven. Sometimes you have not because you ask not."

TAKE THE LIMITS off. Take the lid off." Those two sentences
from the dream wild prophecy echo in my mind. Those *rhema*
words serve as an invisible reminder to keep pressing past what
I think I know so I can break through a demonic glass ceiling that
tries to keep me from soaring in Christ.

We serve a limitless God, but too often we limit Him with
wrong concepts, perceptions, and beliefs about who He is, what
He can do, and what He actually wants to do in our lives. The
world—and sometimes the church—has taught us half-truths or
even lies about what we can be, do, and have in Christ. When we
live, move, and have our being in Him (Acts 17:28), the impossible
becomes possible.

At times we put God in a box, put a lid on that box, and wrap
the box with industrial-strength adhesive tape. Jesus, the breaker,

according to Micah 2:13, wants to break out and break through in our lives, but our unrenewed minds hold us back from realizing our wild dreams. We blame other people. We blame circumstances. Sometimes we even blame the author and finisher of our wild dreams without realizing blame is a guard to change. If we change our minds, we can change our lives. If we change our limiting beliefs to limitless belief in what the Word says, we posture our hearts to receive God's "yes and amen" promises (2 Cor. 1:20).

WHAT THE BIBLE SAYS ABOUT LIMITING BELIEFS

What is a limiting belief? Quite simply, it's a belief that limits you, a thought that talks you out of dreaming wild. The Bible has plenty to say about the way we think. Proverbs 23:7 is one of the most dramatic scriptures about the impact of our thoughts on our physical life I could offer for your consideration: "For as he thinketh in his heart, so is he" (KJV). The Amplified Bible puts it this way, "For as he thinks in his heart, so is he [in behavior...]."

Our thoughts dictate both our speech and our behavior. And what you say and think about yourself impacts you more than what anybody else says and thinks about you. That's why Paul tells us, "Whatever things are true, whatever things are honest, whatever things are just, whatever things are pure, whatever things are lovely, whatever things are of good report, if there is any virtue, and if there is any praise, think on these things" (Phil. 4:8).

Again, the world—and sometimes even the church—has shaped our thinking. Our minds need to be renewed continually because they are continually bombarded by enemy lies. Paul tells us, "Do not be conformed to this world, but be transformed by the renewing of your mind, that you may prove what is the good and acceptable and perfect will of God" (Rom. 12:2). The good and acceptable and perfect will of God includes your wild dreams coming true. But many times our muddied thoughts lead us away from God's clear will.

When the Lord shares with you His dreams about your destiny, it will inspire faith because His words carry within them the faith necessary to believe. But limiting beliefs—or vain imaginations (2 Cor. 10:5)—will soon creep in to dilute your faith. We must identify and resist these vain imaginations because double-mindedness will lead us in the opposite direction of our dreams.

Consider the words of James, the apostle of practical faith: "But let him ask in faith, without wavering. For he who wavers is like a wave of the sea, driven and tossed with the wind. Let not that man think that he will receive anything from the Lord. A double-minded man is unstable in all his ways" (James 1:6–8). We must learn to discern double-mindedness on our journey to dreaming wild.

IDENTIFYING LIMITING BELIEFS

The enemy of your dreams is working overtime to erect a glass ceiling that keeps you from soaring to the heights of God's love for you. Success coach Brian Tracy teaches a principle that can help us break through that invisible lid: "You begin to fly when you let go of self-limiting beliefs and allow your mind and aspirations to rise to greater heights."[1]

What do limiting beliefs sound like? They often begin with words such as "I don't" or "I can't" or "I always" or "I never." Here is a list of common limiting beliefs you need to beware of:

> No matter how hard I try, I never succeed.
> I don't have time to pursue what I really want.
> The resources I need to drive my dream forward are too expensive.
> I don't have enough education to compete in this realm.
> I don't deserve God's best for my life.
> I might fail again.
> I don't have the talent or skills to see my dreams come to pass.
> I am not good at handling finances.

Usually there is subconscious reasoning behind these limiting beliefs. In other words, a "because" follows statements such as these. For example, "No matter how hard I try, I never succeed because I am not educated enough." Or, "I don't follow through because my kids take up every spare moment of my time." Or, "I don't deserve God's best for my life because I make too many mistakes."

When you hear the enemy or your own unrenewed mind telling you why you don't, can't, shouldn't, never, or always do something, make a conscious effort to drill down into the "because." That's the root to which you need to lay an ax with the Word of God. It is God's Word that tells you who you really are and what you can really do in Him. Put another way, the Bible says you can do all things through Christ who strengthens you (Phil. 4:13). If you have a hard time believing that, a lie has crept in to convince you otherwise. That lie is found in the "because."

You may have one major strongman to bind from your mind, or you may have many demon-inspired lies to cast down. Either way, each time you defy a limiting belief, you take one step closer to seeing your God-given dreams come true. The strongman—and every demon power—may be plundering your dreams, but when you bind the work of the enemy in your mind, you set the stage for breaking through the glass ceiling. Jesus explains the concept in Matthew 12:29: "Or else how can one enter a strong man's house and plunder his goods unless he first binds the strong man? And then he will plunder his house."

Most limiting beliefs are rooted in not understanding who you are in Christ or what belongs to you in Him. And they are fueled by some type of fear, however subtle. Consider the following questions to help you identify any limiting beliefs you may have and how they are hindering your wild dreams from coming to pass:

1. What is the biggest accusation you hear against yourself in your own mind?

2. How did this belief creep in? Who introduced this limitation to your life?

3. Is this limiting belief based on even a grain of truth according to God's Word?

4. How is this limiting belief impacting your health, your happiness, your relationships, your finances, and so on?

5. How would overcoming this limiting belief change your life?

Take some time to ponder those questions, asking the Holy Spirit to reveal to you the root causes and give you the courage to challenge wrong thinking with the sword of the Spirit, which is the Word of God (Eph. 6:17). Understanding the battle raging against your mind puts you well on your path to winning the war for your heart.

CHANGING YOUR LIMITING BELIEFS

However subtle or blatant the limiting beliefs are—no matter how great the battle in your mind over your wild dreams is—you can change your mind. We looked at Paul's advice earlier in this chapter, but let's take another look at Romans 12:2 in other translations to drive the point home.

> Do not be conformed to this world (this age), [fashioned after and adapted to its external, superficial customs], but be transformed (changed) by the [entire] renewal of your mind [by its new ideals and its new attitude], so that you may prove [for yourselves] what is the good and acceptable and perfect will of God, even the thing which is good and acceptable and perfect [in His sight for you].
>
> —AMPC

> Don't copy the behavior and customs of this world, but let God transform you into a new person by changing the way you think. Then you will learn to know God's will for you, which is good and pleasing and perfect.
>
> —NLT

Grasping God's wild dream for you often means changing the way you think. When the Lord spoke the dream wild prophecy to me, it was immediately followed by circumstances and situations that challenged my thinking and exposed my limiting beliefs. Here's what I learned in the process.

Write down the limiting beliefs you've discerned, and then make a decision to believe what God's Word says about you instead. Get out a concordance and a Bible, and launch out on a treasure hunt for the truth that will set you free from the enemy's vain imaginations. When you find scriptures that defy your limiting beliefs, write them in a notebook and begin to read them, study them, and confess them.

If you hear thoughts such as "I always stall out before the end" or "I never catch a break" or "I don't have enough money" or "I'm too old, too young, not educated enough" and so on, you need to confess the opposite out of your mouth. For example, confess, "I have endurance because God lives in me; I have the favor of the Lord." Confess, "I can do all things through Christ; I cannot fail because God is on my side." Confess, "I am created in His image; nothing is too hard for God. He supplies."

Begin to decree and declare every day—maybe multiple times a day—what the Word says in defiance of your limiting belief. This is a powerful practice because "the word of God is alive, and active, and sharper than any two-edged sword, piercing even to the division of soul and spirit, of joints and marrow, and able to judge the thoughts and intents of the heart" (Heb. 4:12).

The Word of God will renew your mind—which is part of your soul—so that your soul won't win the war for the desires God has put in your heart. It won't happen overnight, but it will happen. "Jesus said to those Jews who had believed in Him, If you abide in My word [hold fast to My teachings and live in accordance with them], you are truly My disciples. And you will know the Truth, and the Truth will set you free" (John 8:31–32, AMPC).

As you are diligent to think about what you are thinking about, listen carefully to the words coming out of your mouth, and say what God says about you, you will break through the glass ceiling and soar toward God's wild dreams for your life. Mae Jemison, engineer, physician, and NASA astronaut who became the first African American woman to travel in space, is often quoted as saying, "Never limit yourself because of others' limited imagination; never limit others because of your own limited imagination."[2]

DREAM WILD EXERCISE:
STOP UNREASONABLE REASONING

God has given us the ability to reason, but too much mental reasoning blocks spiritual discernment and breeds plenty of confusion. With that in mind, is it possible that you are reasoning yourself out of the full manifestation of your wild dreams? Sometimes we rush out, fully believing we are in God's will, only to run into a major storm that brings discouragement and despair. Then we start to question God. We are confused because we sought wisdom in the counsel of many as we pursued our wild dreams, but we aren't seeing the expected results. Don't let the devil reason you out of your destiny. If you find yourself reasoning, follow the advice in Proverbs 3:5–6: "Trust in the LORD with all your heart, and lean not on your own understanding; in all your ways acknowledge Him, and He will direct your paths."

DROWNING DEATH-LACED WORDS

The Holy Spirit is saying, "If you truly understood the power of your words, it would transform your speech. Father spoke things into existence, and your words will do the same. You are framing the world with the words of your mouth. The power of death and life are in your tongue. I know you have heard this many, many times before, but have you really heard it? I want you to receive revelation and understanding of this life-changing principle. It is a spiritually discerned truth. Do you want this revelation? I'm here to show you."

IT WAS A jaw-dropping moment for me years ago when I asked the Holy Spirit what my biggest problem was and He told me, "Your mouth." I expected Him to tell me I needed to pray more or read the Word more—or do something more. But He assured me my mouth—the very thing He'd called me to use—was my biggest weakness during that season.

To be sure, my mouth worked overtime against the dreams God had in His heart for me. Anytime something went wrong, I would complain, moan, groan, gripe, and otherwise speak against what I knew was God's will for me. I didn't realize I was drowning my dreams with death-laced words until the Holy Spirit led me into this uncomfortable truth.

Upon this surprising revelation, I did what you would do: I started studying scriptures on the mouth so I could align my lips with God's heart. I had already memorized Proverbs 18:21, which says death and life are in the power of the tongue, so I dug deeper. I discovered that if you watch your words and hold your tongue, you'll save yourself a lot of grief (Prov. 21:23, THE MESSAGE.) Here are a few scriptures to consider about how your mouth can stall your wild dreams:

> You are snared with the words of your mouth; you are taken with the words of your mouth.
> —PROVERBS 6:2

> A man will be satisfied with good by the fruit of his mouth, and the recompense of a man's hands will be rendered to him.
> —PROVERBS 12:14

> He who guards his mouth preserves his life, but he who opens wide his lips will have destruction.
> —PROVERBS 13:3

> A man has joy by the answer of his mouth, and a word spoken in due season, how good it is!
> —PROVERBS 15:23

> The heart of the righteous studies to answer, but the mouth of the wicked pours out evil things.
> —PROVERBS 15:28

> The heart of the wise teaches his mouth, and adds learning to his lips.
> —PROVERBS 16:23

> A fool's lips enter into contention, and his mouth calls for flogging.
> —PROVERBS 18:6

The more I studied, the more foolish I felt as the conviction of the Holy Spirit fell upon me. Of course the enemy saw the weakness and set out to exploit it so he could serve up a plate of cold condemnation after I fell into his wicked trap time and time again. Nevertheless, I set my heart to cooperate with the Holy Spirit to tame my tongue in the midst of the war against my mind and eventually gained ground.

THE WAR FOR OUR WORDS

The weapons of our warfare are not carnal but mighty in God for the pulling down of strongholds in our minds (2 Cor. 10:14). But the weapons of Satan are carnal, mighty in our flesh for the erecting of strongholds in our minds—and we're the ones arming him to kill, steal, and destroy our dreams before they ever come true.

Jesus "disarmed authorities and powers, He made a show of them openly, triumphing over them by the cross" (Col. 2:15). Many who oppose spiritual warfare practices point to that scripture and say we don't have to fight because the devil is already defeated. Yes, the enemy of your wild dreams is technically already defeated, but Paul nevertheless told Timothy to "fight the good fight of faith" (1 Tim. 6:12), and he told the Ephesians we wrestle "against principalities, against powers, against the rulers of the darkness of this world, and against spiritual forces of evil in the heavenly places" (Eph. 6:12).

If Jesus disarmed principalities and powers, why are we still wrestling with them to see our dreams manifest? We still wrestle in part because we are arming the enemy with the words of our mouths, handing him our God-given authority to use against us. Satan has no authority over us unless we give it to him, just as the serpent had no authority in the garden until Adam gave it to him.

As I was meditating on 2 Corinthians 10:4 one day, I received a revelation about our words being weapons. This is not a positive confession revelation, though I believe in confessing what the Word of God says rather than confessing negative thoughts and feelings. That's totally scriptural. No, this is not a new twist on a good confession. This is a spiritual warfare strategy that will send the devil fleeing as we submit our words to God and resist the temptation to allow our mouths to issue weapons Satan uses against us.

When discussing the whole armor of God, Paul instructs us to take the sword of the Spirit, which is the Word of God (Eph. 6:17). When we speak the Word of God out of our mouths, it serves as a weapon that cuts through every evil plot of the enemy against our dreams. No devil in hell can come against the Word of God because it's not carnal but mighty—supernatural—in God.

THREE COMMON MOUTH MISTAKES

Yet when we find ourselves in the midst of the battle for our dreams, we too often make one of three common mistakes: (1) We fail to wield the sword of the Spirit, which is the Word of God; (2) we speak the enemy's fearful lies about our dreams out of our mouths; or (3) we are double-minded, speaking the Word of God one moment and the enemy's fear-laced lies the next. The only sure way to enforce Jesus's victory in our lives is to consistently wield the sword of the Spirit.

Let's look at each option and how it works.

Wielding the sword of the Spirit

First, when we wield the sword of the Spirit, we are packing a powerful weapon. The writer of Hebrews says, "For the word of God is alive, and active, and sharper than any two-edged sword, piercing even to the division of soul and spirit, of joints and marrow, and able to judge the thoughts and intents of the heart" (Heb. 4:12).

The sword of the Spirit is sharper than any natural sword. It has supernatural power, but we have to speak out the living power it contains with our tongues. Inspired by the life-giving Holy Spirit, the wisest man on the earth once wrote, "Death and life are in the power of the tongue, and those who love it will eat its fruit" (Prov. 18:21).

Speaking God's Word instead of the enemy's lies

Our words are weapons. When we speak God's Word out of our mouths, it casts out death and opens the door to life in our situations. When we make the mistake of speaking the enemy's fearful lies out of our mouths—which may sound like worry, doubt, unbelief, or something other than the pure truth—we are allowing the enemy to use our own words as weapons against us.

Again, the devil's weapons are carnal in the sense that he works through our carnal nature to oppress us by successfully tempting us to speak death with our powerful tongues. We essentially arm the enemy with weapons of death and give him some ammunition to oppress us when we speak words that are out of alignment with God's truth.

Refusing to be double-minded

When we are double-minded, speaking the Word of God one moment and the enemy's fearful lies the next, we allow the enemy to take ground in our lives. Have you ever felt as if you were taking one step forward and two steps back? This is often the result of double-mindedness. We speak life out of our mouths, penetrating the enemy's plans with the sword of the Spirit in the morning, but as soon as we see a circumstance that doesn't go our way, we once again arm the enemy with carnal weapons through our words.

The Bible says, "A double-minded man is unstable in all his ways" (James 1:8). If you are feeling unstable, as if the enemy is tossing you around a wrestling ring and about to capture you in a figure-four, it may be because you are not speaking words of faith and life. Instead, you may be arming the enemy with words of fear, doubt, unbelief, and death.

Here's the revelation in summary: Your words are weapons in spiritual warfare. When you speak the Word of God, you are wielding a sword that will devastate the enemy's evil plans. It may take more than one swing, but if you keep swinging your supernatural sword, you will see natural results. When you speak words based on thoughts and fears the enemy sows in your soul, you are essentially arming the enemy with carnal words that breed death. You give life to what you speak. Will you give life to God's plan or to the enemy's? It's up to you.

Mother Teresa put it this way: "Words which do not give the light of Christ increase the darkness."[1]

DREAM WILD EXERCISE: LISTEN TO YOURSELF

Research shows it takes at least twenty-one days to develop a new habit. Ask the Holy Spirit to help you hyper-focus on your words for the next three weeks. The goal here is to root out the power of death—to disarm the enemy by refusing to complain, moan, groan, gripe, grumble, grouse, criticize, lament, whine, bellyache, fuss, or release negative words of any sort. You may be surprised to hear what comes out of your mouth! When you hear yourself releasing the power of death over your dreams, immediately repent, ask the Lord to help you hold your tongue, and release life over your wild dreams instead. Do this repeatedly, and soon enough it will become supernaturally natural to you.

DAY 8

FIGHTING FEAR'S FIERCE AGENDA

The Holy Spirit is saying, "Fear is a manifestation of the enemy's lies. Satan is the father of lies, the father of fear, the father of destruction and devastation. I have not and will not give you a spirit of fear. I have given you a spirit of power to overcome the fear that's trying to overcome you. I have given you My love that combats every feeling of fear. I have given you a sound mind to discern the subtle voice of fear that speaks against your dreams. Don't allow yourself to fear for even a second. Call out to Me, and My love will deliver you from every fear."

WHEN GOD DROPS a wild dream in your heart, the enemy always counters with fearful thoughts designed to dismantle your daring desires. Fear almost immediately makes moves against your mind in the form of imaginations that drive unreasonable reasonings. Many times fear serves as a giant in your life that stands between you and your Promised Land.

Left unchecked, fearful imaginations eventually produce an emotion that ignites a process of paralysis by analysis. Dreadful "what-ifs" lead you into confusion, and overthinking stops you from driving toward your dream. As the Bible says, fear has torment (1 John 4:18, KJV).

God doesn't want us to fear—not even a little. That's because fear contaminates our faith. We can't move in faith and move in fear at the same time—and faith is the currency of the kingdom. When you cast down fearful imaginations, you suddenly see clearly how unreasonable the enemy's subtle suggestions about your life really are—and you can run toward your dream again.

God didn't give you a spirit of fear—but that doesn't mean fear isn't harassing you. You may know you have fear—or fear may be deceiving you with its wily whispers and sneaky strongholds in your soul. The good news is those anxieties that have plagued you—those dreadful voices that have prophesied to you—must bow in the name of Jesus!

MY DELIVERANCE FROM FEAR

Fear once had such a tight grip on my soul that if an email came that I thought offered bad news, I closed my eyes, held my breath, forwarded it to a friend, and asked her to read it and tell me what it said. One time I ordered pizza on a Friday night. When the delivery boy knocked on the door forty-five minutes later, it scared me so much I locked myself in my bedroom. Then I called to complain that the pizza never showed up!

Fear was a bondage that affected every area of my life. But fear is not always so obvious. I did some research and discovered a phobia list. There are literally dozens of diagnosed phobias. Some are common, and some are so ridiculous you know the devil has to be at work. Some of the ridiculous phobias are fear of flowers, fear of eyes, fear of numbers, fear of ugliness, fear of books, fear of teenagers, fear of mirrors, fear of cooking, and fear of clocks.[1]

I'll always remember the episode of *Maury* during which he interviewed a woman who was scared of pickles. Another lady on the episode was afraid of cotton balls—she said they made a noise.[2] These unreasonable fears were literally ruining their lives. You and I aren't dealing with anything so ridiculous. But we could be dealing with subtle fears that are robbing us of God's dream for our lives.

There are many other "fear ofs" we may not even know we face, such as fear of failure, fear of lack, fear of success, fear of disappointing people, fear of losing a job, fear of loneliness, fear of making decisions, fear of conflict, fear of rejection, fear of losing relationships, and so on.

Fear is the most difficult to overcome when its influence is so subtle it's hard to trace a behavior to the root of fear. Fear, after all, is an invisible enemy. If you have certain fears, you may not even know it because your coping mechanism—your response to fear—has become part of your personality. When fear influences you, you take action based on your fear instead of your faith. You keep failing because you don't have the faith to succeed. You won't make a decision because you're afraid you didn't hear from God. You won't try to make new friends because you're afraid of rejection. You won't sow because you fear lack. And on and on it goes.

CASTING DOWN FEARFUL IMAGINATIONS

Paul taught us the concept of casting down imaginations, but many believers don't understand how to engage in this type of mind warfare. Second Corinthians 10:5 lays out the concept: "Casting down imaginations and every high thing that exalts itself against the knowledge of God, bringing every thought into captivity to the obedience of Christ."

The classic edition of the Amplified Bible breaks it down in finer detail: "[Inasmuch as we] refute arguments and theories and reasonings and every proud and lofty thing that sets itself up against the [true] knowledge of God; and we lead every thought and purpose away captive into the obedience of Christ (the Messiah, the Anointed One)."

As we seek to cast down fearful imaginations—or any imaginations that exalt themselves against the knowledge of God—it's helpful to understand that the phrase *casting down* in that verse comes from the Greek word *kathaireō*, which has a violent connotation. It means to "forcibly yank down; destroy, leaving nothing 'standing' or even in good working order; cast down."[3] It also means "with the use of force: to throw down, cast down."[4]

We must purpose in our hearts not to allow any trace of fearful thoughts to linger in our minds. The Bible says we are to cast down *every* imagination, not some imaginations. The battle is in your mind, but the war is for your heart. When fierce, fear-based thoughts come against you, you must decide to evict them with the full force of your will. That begins by paying attention to your thought life. You have to think about what you are thinking about.

Here's a practical example. Let's say you hear a thought such as "What if I pursue my heart's desire and look like a fool when I fall flat on my face?" You know that's not the Lord speaking to you. The Holy Spirit does not speak to you in terms of failure because there is no failure in Christ. If the Holy Spirit was trying to warn you that you were on the wrong path, He would speak to you in peaceable wisdom, not with fearful thoughts. Fear is not the way of God.

So if you hear a fearful thought such as the previous example, you must first recognize the thought as a vain imagination that is exalting itself above God's Word and God's dream for your life. Next, you have to take that thought captive. Out of your holy mouth, you would say, "I reject the thought that I will fall flat on my face and look like a fool. I bind that vain imagination in the name of Jesus." But it's not enough to stop there. You also need to speak the opposite out of your mouth according to the Word of God. In this case you would say, "No one who hopes in the Lord will ever be put to shame (Ps. 25:3). I put my trust in the Lord who always leads me into triumph in Christ Jesus (2 Cor. 2:14). I thank You, Lord, that You give me confidence to pursue the dreams You have put in my heart, in Jesus's name."

The idea is you never cast down without lifting up the Word of God. You don't bind without loosing. You don't just eradicate a wrong thought. You replace it with the right thought. You may have to do this over and over again with fearful thoughts because we never defeat fear once and for all. Fear is always roaming about like a roaring lion, looking to devour your wild dreams. But you can submit yourself to God, resist fear, and force it to flee (James 4:7).

THE OVERARCHING ANSWER TO FEAR

The Holy Spirit told me this: "When you have a healthy fear of the Lord, you become so consumed with pleasing Him—you become so full of faith in His power—that there is literally no room for the devil's fear tactics."

When we have a healthy fear of the Lord, we won't take thought to his suggestions because we believe God! I'm scared *not* to believe

God! Fear is part of the curse of the law. (See Deuteronomy 28:66.) Jesus redeemed us from the curse of the law (Gal. 3:13). God has not given us a spirit of fear, but of power, love, and a sound mind (2 Tim. 1:7). Fear dilutes your power, causes you to doubt God's love—that perfect love that casts out fear—and makes your mind unsound. Reverent, worshipful fear of the Lord carries a revelation of the love of God. It carries a revelation of the power of God. It carries a revelation of the truth of God's Word. It's all wrapped up in the fear of the Lord!

I challenge you today to meditate on the fear of the Lord. Fear is a fierce enemy, but your God is fiercer than any spirit of fear. "If God is for us, who can be against us?" (Rom. 8:31). Jeremiah 20:11 says, "But GOD, a most fierce warrior, is at my side. Those who are after me will be sent sprawling—slapstick buffoons falling all over themselves, a spectacle of humiliation no one will ever forget" (THE MESSAGE). And Nahum 1:2 assures us, "GOD is serious business. He won't be trifled with. He avenges his foes. He stands up against his enemies, fierce and raging" (THE MESSAGE). Amen!

Let these words from Joyce Meyer inspire you: "The eagle has no fear of adversity. We need to be like the eagle and have a fearless spirit of a conqueror!"[5]

DREAM WILD EXERCISE: DISCERNING FEAR IN YOUR HEART

Take some time right now to consider whether fear is combating your wild dreams. When you settle for something rather than pressing into what you feel called to do, that's a sign of fear. Likewise, when you criticize someone else's wild dream pursuits, it could be fear rising in your heart. Procrastination can be rooted in fear. Feeling anxiety over making a decision is grounded in fear. You could even have physical symptoms of fear such as a racing heart, trouble concentrating, a feeling of overwhelm, or insomnia. Discern fear and root it out through prayer and by renewing your mind with the Word of God.

DISCONNECTING WRONG ALIGNMENTS

The Holy Spirit is saying, "I will bring people across your path to help you accomplish what I have called you to do. I will help you make the connections— and connect the dots. Yes, I will direct your steps toward the people, places, and things you need to reach your destiny in Christ. That is My part and My joy. Your part is to ask Me, to seek Me, to hear Me, and to follow and obey Me. We are in this together. I will do My part. You must do your part."

ALIGNMENTS—THOSE PEOPLE you submit to, run with, or are otherwise in close connection with—affect your life in ways you may not have considered. I learned this a few years ago when I had a roach infestation in my condo.

I saw one roach, then two, then five. I called in the exterminator to spray and headed out on my next ministry trip. When I came back, there were even more roaches. There were roaches in my computer printer, roaches in my coffee maker—yes, disgusting, I know. There were roaches in the drains. There were roaches everywhere.

Now, there was no natural reason for this. My teenaged daughter had moved out of the house, so there weren't any Cheetos between the couch cushions or empty ice cream bowls under the bed. My maid service came frequently, and so did the exterminator. I was frustrated and set out to kill those buggers for good with a toxic bomb that releases so much poison you have to leave your house for hours after you set it off.

The bug bomb was successful—for about a day. But when I returned from my next ministry trip, the roaches were once again everywhere. I called my condo association and insisted they get to the bottom of the issue. They sent out an exterminator again, but nothing changed. Finally, I was at my wits' end and demanded a solution. Management dispatched another exterminator, who finally discovered the source of the infestation.

As it turns out, the neighbors above me—what we call snow birds because they live in their condo only a few times a year—had an infestation in their unit. I didn't see the state of their apartment, but the exterminator told me roaches were crawling everywhere— I mean *everywhere*. Because my condo shared a wall with their condo, the roaches were climbing down into my condo. Since the exterminators eradicated the roaches from my neighbors above, I haven't seen so much as a single roach.

Through that experience, the Lord showed me how critical alignments are. Essentially I was paying a price for the negligence of my neighbors. Offering a spiritual angle to the issue, I was taking massive warfare for their sin. Because of the direct connection, what they did was clearly affecting me even though my house was clean.

Relational alignments are the same way. If you are aligned with someone who is persistently practicing sin, it affects you. If you are aligned with someone who has a negative mind-set, it affects you. If you are aligned with someone who is handling money improperly, it affects you. Conversely, if you are aligned with someone who is walking in holiness, it influences you. If you are aligned with someone who has a powerful healing or prophetic ministry, you benefit from that. If you are aligned with someone who is on fire for God, that impacts you.

What I've also learned is you can have wrong alignments with good people—people who are holy, loving, and on fire for God, but if it's not a God alignment, it's a wrong alignment. Put another way, it can be a distraction. Every good thing is not a God thing. God has right alignments—divine connections—for you. If we spend all our energy working with good people without a God-ordained alignment, we could miss the Holy Spirit relationships that move us faster toward our destiny.

BAD COMPANY CORRUPTS WILD DREAMS

Motivational speaker Jim Rohn once said, "You're the average of the five people you spend most of your time with."[1] The idea here is the people who are closest to us have the most influence over us. Our parents have the most influence over us as children. Our friends usually have the most sway in our lives as teenagers. Our coworkers and those we fellowship with tend to have the most pull on us as adults. With this in mind, let's explore what the Bible says about our alignments in the context of dreaming wild.

Avoid bad company

First Corinthians 15:33 says, "Do not be deceived: 'Bad company corrupts good morals.'" In the context of dreaming wild, you might say naysayers corrupt godly aspirations. If you hang out with Debbie Downer and Negative Nancy, you could find your faith failing you at the moment of launch. Align yourself with people who will support your wild dreams, even and especially in the midst of obstacles, delays, and wild warfare.

Don't be unequally yoked

Second Corinthians 6:14–15 tells us, "Do not be unequally yoked together with unbelievers. For what fellowship has righteousness with unrighteousness? What communion has light with darkness? What agreement has Christ with Belial? Or what part has he who believes with an unbeliever?" As you set out to take faith-inspired actions toward your wild dreams, be careful whom you partner with. It's not wise to engage in joint ventures with unbelievers, even if they are friends and family.

What many don't realize, though, is you can also be unequally yoked with believers. If your faith levels are vastly different, that yoke can hold you back. If there is habitual sin in a believer's life, the person's bondage could weigh you down. If your capacity to run is far greater than your Christian partner's, he or she could slow you down to the point that you miss a God-ordained opportunity waiting for the person to complete responsibilities.

Avoid those who cause division

Romans 16:17 says, "Now I urge you, brothers, to closely watch those who cause divisions and offenses, contrary to the teaching which you have learned, and avoid them." Strife kills the anointing. If you align yourself with someone who is offended, causes divisions, or sows seeds of discord among the brethren, which is an abomination to the Lord (Prov. 6:16–19), you are setting yourself up for unnecessary warfare. There will be warfare enough along the road to seeing your wildest of wild dreams come true. You don't need to open the door by aligning with a divisive person.

Walk with the wise

Proverbs 13:20 warns, "He who walks with wise men will be wise, but a companion of fools will be destroyed." Proverbs 16:29 cautions us, "A violent man entices his neighbor, and leads him into the way that is not good." And Proverbs 22:24–25 admonishes us: "Make no friendship with an angry man, and with a furious man you will not go, lest you learn his ways and get a snare to your soul."

As you pursue right alignments, keep Psalm 1:1–4 in mind: "Blessed is the man who walks not in the counsel of the ungodly nor stands in the path of sinners, nor sits in the seat of scoffers; but his delight is in the law of the LORD, and in His law he meditates day and night. He will be like a tree planted by the rivers of water, that brings forth its fruit in its season; its leaf will not wither, and whatever he does will prosper. The ungodly are not so, but are like the chaff which the wind drives away."

LOOK FOR THE DIVINE CONNECTIONS

As we take caution to discern alignments that hinder, we should also stay sensitive to the Holy Spirit's leading to recognize divine connections—or divine reconnections. Divine connections are God-breathed relationships that seemingly come out of nowhere and have the potential to radically impact your life—and they are vital to fulfilling Father's call on your life. To be sure, these relationships can be absolutely life-changing, even if they are only for a season.

Divine connections are scriptural and necessary. Moses and

Joshua had a divine connection. Samuel and David had a divine connection. Elijah and Elisha had a divine connection. Paul and Timothy had a divine connection. In each case we see destiny arising from those relationships. Joshua took the Promised Land baton from Moses. Samuel anointed David as king. Elisha grabbed Elijah's mantle. And Timothy carried on Paul's gospel mission.

Again, divine connections often spring up seemingly out of nowhere. Only it's not out of nowhere. It's what I call a "suddenly." *Merriam-Webster* defines *suddenly* as "happening or coming unexpectedly; changing angle or character all at once; marked by or manifesting abruptness or haste; made or brought about in a short time."[2]

Just days after I received the dream wild prophecy, I found myself ministering in Texas. I felt as if death warmed over, and I could barely think straight. My neck was aching, my head was pounding, and my body was sore. I pressed on to keep my word to preach because I've learned that what the enemy can use to stop you, he'll keep using over and over again to defeat you.

I preached on transition and apparently walked up to a couple on the second row and said, "I like you." I don't even remember it, honestly, but when I said those words, the couple were hit with Holy Spirit inspiration to reach out to me about working on some branding efforts for the ministry. They reached out on a Facebook account I rarely check, and I agreed to hop on a call with a stranger, which I rarely do because I'm literally flooded with these types of requests.

To make a very long story short, less than six months later we're doing mighty kingdom exploits together, the likes of which I could never have imagined. After years of doing the best I could with what I had, the Lord sent me a couple who believes in my dreams as much as I do, and we're dreaming wild together—and seeing massive fruit.

DISCERNING DIVINE RECONNECTIONS

I'm grateful for the many divine connections God has brought into my life. I've been blessed with many godly relationships that have strengthened me, opened doors for me, and imparted wisdom that would have otherwise taken me decades to glean. In recent years, though, God has put an emphasis on divine reconnections in my life that have been as powerful as any divine connection I've ever experienced.

Indeed, I've seen three especially significant divine reconnections that have brought spiritual increase into my life I wasn't expecting and could never have walked into on my own two feet. One of them was with Ryan LeStrange. Together we founded awakeningtv.com, and he is now my fellow New Breed Revival Network leader. After a decade we reconnected some years ago, and it has been explosive.

Another divine reconnection was with Rich and Dottie Kane of the Healing Rooms Ministries of South Florida. They have stood with me, walked by me, and helped me launch Awakening Healing Rooms at the Awakening House of Prayer in Hollywood, Florida. During the training session a woman came in with terminal cancer, seeking prayer. We prayed for her, the power of God overtook her, and the doctors could not explain how her cancer markers dropped from 16 to 1.5. It was God—and through a divine reconnection.

For all the divine connections I see in the Bible, I also see powerful divine reconnections, or full-circle relationships in Scripture that reveal God's redemptive, reconciliatory power. One of the most powerful divine reconnections is Paul's relationship with John Mark. When Saul and Barnabas set out to the mission field, they took young John Mark with them (Acts 12:25). For whatever reason (likely connected to the spiritual warfare that raged against Paul's ministry), John Mark abandoned the mission (Acts 13:13).

Later, Saul and Barnabas split because Barnabas wanted to take John Mark with them, but Paul thought it was better not to take him since he bailed the first time around. But God brought the relationship full circle. In one of Paul's last letters from prison he mentioned John Mark, telling his spiritual son Timothy to "get Mark, and bring him with you, for he is profitable to me for the ministry" (2 Tim. 4:11).[3]

Lot also experienced a divine reconnection with Abraham that may have saved his life. Lot and his family were taken captive by five kings (Gen. 14:8–12). When Abraham heard it, he gathered 318 men from his household and set out to rescue Lot—and succeeded (Gen. 14:14–16). Although they did not continue walking together as they had before—Lot chose to dwell in Sodom—it was a powerful, divine reconnection.

Just as it is with divine connections, you can't make divine reconnections happen. That's part of the reason they are called divine. It is God's doing in His way and with His timing. When they do come, full-circle relationships manifest in His season and for His reason. I believe in this season God is bringing forth many divine reconnections and also breathing new life into established relationships so we can run swiftly into His purposes and redeem the time because the days are evil. Dream wild!

President George Washington once said, "It is better to be alone than in bad company."[4] And the good news is you are not alone. The Holy Spirit is your constant companion.

DREAM WILD EXERCISE:
DISCERNING RIGHT AND WRONG ALIGNMENTS

With regard to false prophets, Jesus said, "You will know them by their fruit. Do men gather grapes from thorns, or figs from this-tles? Even so, every good tree bears good fruit. But a corrupt tree bears evil fruit. A good tree cannot bear evil fruit, nor can a cor-rupt tree bear good fruit" (Matt. 7:16–18). The same could be said for alignments. You will know good alignments by their fruit. If people you are aligned with cause nothing but drama, warfare, and misery, you must question how closely you are to walk with them—if at all. When God brings divine connections in your life, increase follows. That doesn't mean there will never be conflict or misun-derstanding, but the good should far outweigh the bad. Take some time to consider the fruit of your relationships. Are they moving you toward or away from your dreams?

PRESSING PAST FAILURES

*The Holy Spirit is saying, "I know you feel weak
on some days. Rejoice. My strength is made perfect
in your weakness. Your weakness does not surprise
or disappoint Me. I knew you would not always
win your inner battles with temptation when I
wooed you into this relationship. You are a work
in progress, but I see you as a masterpiece despite
your failures. I see you as a winner. I see you
through the eyes of love. I see you through the
blood of Jesus. So call upon Me to strengthen you,
and I will help you overcome your weaknesses."*

WHEN I JOINED the college newspaper, I had dreamed of becoming the editor. I started out as a reporter, worked my way up to news editor, then features editor, then managing editor. But the dream of editorship eluded me. It wasn't because I wasn't talented enough or didn't work hard enough. It was mere politics. The girl who held the editorship was vying for a scholarship to a major journalism school, so the publisher gave her the title even though I did all her work.

When I finally grew tired of carrying the entire load, I ventured out to launch my own student body newspaper. With a small team of past graduates, we put together a fully funded paper that turned the heads of the college administration. Our newspaper surpassed the quality in writing, graphics, and photography of the official school paper. We had full support as an alternative newspaper on campus, and my dream came true.

I celebrated for a moment. I was on top of the world. But I soon discovered I could not sustain a monthly paper with a small staff and even smaller budget while also working a full-time job and pursuing an education. I published only one issue of our paper and for the next year felt like a miserable failure. That perceived failure—and I say perceived because I was the only one who saw it as a failure—spun me into a depressive state. I felt as if my dream had died.

Eventually I had to press past that failure and move on. If I hadn't—if I had let that setback stop me—I would never have risen through the ranks of the publishing world to achieve even wilder dreams than editing a college newspaper. In my youth I didn't understand that everybody fails sometimes while going after dreams. Indeed, some of the greatest men in world and Bible history failed miserably as they journeyed toward their wild dreams. What sets those great men and women apart from the ones we don't read about is they didn't let failure define them—they let it teach them.

HOW GOD VIEWS OUR FAILURES

God views failure differently from the way most people view failure. While God hates sin, our failures are not necessarily sin. Failure in itself is not sin, unless it's a failure manifesting from sin. Put another way, just because you fail to see your dream come true doesn't mean you are a failure. The timing could be off. The enemy could have reared his ugly head. You may have lacked some skill to drive the dream forward. In the context of pursuing your dreams, you only fail if you quit and give up.

Proverbs 24:16 tells us, "A just man falls seven times and rises up again." No matter how many times you need to pick yourself up and dust yourself off, it will all be worth it when you see your God-given dreams come true—and they will if you refuse to quit. When you stumble and fall—when you make a mistake along the road to your dreams—let Micah 7:8 be your declaration: "Do not rejoice over me, my enemy! Although I have fallen, I will rise; although I dwell in darkness, the LORD is my light."

If you are pressing past failures, let these scriptures encourage your heart:

> The steps of a man are made firm by the LORD; He delights in his way. Though he falls, he will not be hurled down, for the LORD supports him with His hand.
> —PSALM 37:23–24

> The LORD upholds all who fall, and raises up all who are bowed down.
> —PSALM 145:14

> My flesh and my heart fails, but God is the strength of my heart and my portion forever.
> —PSALM 73:26

> Do not remember the former things nor consider the things of old.
> —ISAIAH 43:18

IT'S JUST A SETBACK—IT'S NOT YOUR FUTURE

"It's just a setback; it's not your future." I remember when the Holy Spirit spoke those words to me some years ago. I had just experienced a devastating blow—a one-two (-three-four) punch from the enemy. It sent me reeling with a spinning head and wobbling legs. Let's just say I never saw it coming. My wild dream looked as dead as the proverbial doornail.

But when the Holy Spirit spoke those eight simple words to me, the spiritual oppression that was trying to settle on my soul broke. I suddenly had an all-new, more hopeful perspective. Instead of focusing on my immediate past, I began to look for the next step in God's dream for my future.

Have you encountered a setback to your wild dreams, something unexpected that spoiled your plans and disappointed your heart? It could be a failed relationship, a financial calamity, a health issue. Beloved, see this setback for what it is. Setbacks are delays. Setbacks are hindrances. But setbacks are not necessarily failures. You did not fail because you encountered defeat. You fail only when you choose not to get back up and keep going. It's just a setback. It's not your future.

I like to put it this way: a setback is a form of feedback. In other words, when you encounter a setback, it should cause you to stop and assess your situation. How did you come to this point? Could you have done something differently? How should you respond now? Stop, look, listen, and learn from the Holy Spirit, and you will find wisdom that will help you avoid similar setbacks in the future God has for you.

Henry Ford, founder of the Ford Motor Company, once said: "Life is a series of experiences, each one of which makes us bigger, even though sometimes it is hard to realize this. For the world was built to develop character, and we must learn that the setbacks and griefs which we endure help us in our marching onward."[1]

There are countless books on great men and women who faced setbacks on the way to realizing their dreams. Michael Jordan was cut from his high school basketball team.[2] Setback. Thomas Edison failed a thousand times to invent the light bulb before he found success.[3] Setback. Walt Disney was fired from a newspaper for not being creative enough.[4] Setback. Steve Jobs was fired from Apple.[5] Setback.

Despite the setbacks—all of them rather humiliating—each went on to make his mark on modern history by realizing his wild dreams. None of these men allowed his setback to become his future. Instead, they turned their mistakes into a coach. Imagine if they hadn't. You have something to contribute to the world. Don't let your setbacks define your future.

RECOVERING FROM SETBACKS

I've seen my fair share of setbacks to my dreams—and then some. One was a financial devastation. I had an enviable gig with a major broadcaster running editorial operations on a popular small-business website. I was riding high, making the big bucks and sure that my future was bright. Then it happened. The dot-com bubble burst, and the contract vanished in the twinkling of an eye. All of my proverbial eggs were in a single basket. Setback.

I had two choices: recover or starve. I didn't have time to wallow in the shock. I had to let the mistake of putting all my eggs in one basket become a coach. It taught me the value of diversification. Instead of one revenue stream, I now have multiple revenue streams from various sources so that if one bubbling brook dries up, there's another to keep the finances flowing freely.

You may never face anything as devastating as divorce or job loss, but even minor setbacks can derail you if you don't keep the right perspective. How do you recover? Again, remember that it's just a setback. It's not your future. American author Les Brown once said, "Anytime you suffer a setback or disappointment, put your head down and plow ahead."[6] And Harry S. Truman said, "I've had a few setbacks in my life, but I never gave up."[7]

I've had plenty of setbacks in my life—from abandonment and divorce to betrayal and imprisonment. I would have lost heart unless I had believed that I would see the goodness of the Lord in the land of the living. (See Psalm 27:13.) I would have given up if I hadn't embraced the fact that the setbacks were just that—setbacks. It's just a setback. It's not your future.

So stop focusing on the past—even if the past was this morning—and focus on Him. Paul the apostle faced setbacks. But he pressed on to lay hold of that for which Christ Jesus laid hold of him, and he did it by looking ahead: "Brothers, I do not count myself to have attained, but this one thing I do, forgetting those things which are behind and reaching forward to those things which are ahead, I press toward the goal to the prize of the high calling of God in Christ Jesus" (Phil. 3:13–14). So remember, it's just a setback. It's not your future. God is still on the throne.

To quote the famous saying, "Success is not final, failure is not fatal: it is the courage to continue that counts."[8]

DREAM WILD EXERCISE:
ENCOURAGE YOURSELF IN THE LORD

Failure—even if it's perceived failure—is discouraging. When David and his men returned to Ziglag, the Amalekites had burned down their camp and kidnapped their wives and children. David's men wept and wanted to stone him. First Samuel 30:6 says, "David encouraged himself in the LORD." I believe that in this time of perceived failure and defeat, David reminded himself of the past victories he had experienced in God. He remembered when he defeated the lion and the bear in the wilderness and Goliath in the valley. When you feel down and out over a failure or defeat, remind yourself of past victories instead of meditating on current failures.

FIGHTING OFF FRUSTRATIONS

The Holy Spirit is saying, "Getting frustrated takes
you nowhere fast—except into anxiety, anger, and
all manner of ungodly reactions. When you sense
that you are getting frustrated, you have stopped
receiving My grace. Don't move ahead of Me, and
don't question My ability. Take a deep breath and
know that I'm going to work it out, whether it's a
difficult assignment, an annoying person, or some
pain in your body. Let go of the frustration, and
receive My grace to empower you to move toward your
goal. I believe in you, and what frustrates you doesn't
frustrate Me. Let My peace overcome you now."

FRUSTRATION. SOME PEOPLE experience it now and then, and some people wrestle with it day after day as they pursue their dreams with a passion. You may be frustrated right now. *Merriam-Webster* defines *frustration* as "a feeling of anger or annoyance caused by being unable to do something: the state of being frustrated" and "a deep chronic sense or state of insecurity and dissatisfaction arising from unresolved problems or unfulfilled needs."[1]

You might be frustrated with your spouse for not meeting your dreamy expectations. You could be frustrated with your boss for not giving you the dream promotion he promised. You may be frustrated with yourself for not losing those ten pounds you set out to shed last year—and even putting on a few. You could be frustrated about all these things and more, but it doesn't do you a bit of good—in fact, frustration breeds more frustration and delays the manifestation of your dream.

TRADING FLESHLY FRUSTRATION FOR GOD'S GRACE

I'll admit it. I have been prone to frustration, even over small things. I've been frustrated over flight delays that caused me to lose a night's sleep, frustrated over the air conditioning in my office going out and leaving me sweating on deadline, frustrated about those stubborn ten pounds, frustrated over the actions of people who generally make my life harder for no good reason, and so on and so on and so on.

What I learned was this: the devil wants to keep us in a constant state of frustration because we cannot operate in the grace of God and frustration at the same time any more than we can operate in faith and fear at the same time. Paul warned us not to frustrate the grace of God (Gal. 2:21, KJV). We need mega grace to see our mega dreams come true. It's His power in us that helps us persevere.

The Greek word for grace in that verse is *charis*, which is translated to mean "grace, that which affords joy, pleasure, delight, sweetness, charm, loveliness; grace of speech; good will, lovingkindness, favor; of a merciful kindness by which God, exerting His holy influence upon souls, turns them to Christ, keeps, strengthens, increases them in Christian faith, knowledge, affection, and kindles them to the exercise of the Christian virtues; the spiritual condition of one governed by the power of divine grace; thanks, recompense, reward."[2]

I don't know about you, but I'll take grace over frustration any day.

When we're frustrated, we're frustrating the grace of God because God's grace is available to help us, but we're too focused on outward circumstances (or inward thoughts) to focus on Him. We know the scripture: God will keep you in perfect peace if you keep your mind set on Him (Isa. 26:3). If we put our faith on that and take action, we will not operate in frustration—we will receive grace to help in time of need.

CAST YOUR FRUSTRATIONS ON HIM

Surely you've read the verse "Cast all your care on Him, because He cares for you" (1 Pet. 5:7). What is a frustration, ultimately, but a care? What would happen if instead of frustrating or blocking the grace of God from operating in our lives, we cast the frustrations and tap into the grace to pursue our wild dreams?

Beyond keeping our eyes on the author and finisher of our faith, the best way to do this, I've found, is to use our faith in prayer. What if you turned every frustration, each time it arose, into a prayer request? What if, when you felt that familiar feeling of frustration begin to rise up in your soul, you put your faith on Philippians 4:6: "Be anxious for nothing, but in everything, by prayer and supplication with gratitude, make your requests known to God"?

Frustration left unchecked ultimately causes anxiety. Why not stop frustration dead in its tracks before it gets to that point? Why not be frustrated for nothing, but in everything, by prayer and supplication with gratitude ask God to work it out—or give you the wisdom and grace to walk it out?

When you are frustrated with your boss for not giving you that promotion, why not pray: "Father, I'm grateful that I have a job and that You are my provider. I trust You for the right promotion at the right time, and I believe You for increase in my life." Instead of acting in frustration with your kids, why not pray instead?

When you do, the second half of Philippians 4:7 can manifest in your life: "The peace of God, which surpasses all understanding, will protect your hearts and minds through Christ Jesus." When you are peaceful, you can receive abundant grace.

So again, turn your frustrations into prayer requests, and you will walk in grace and peace that confuses your enemies and blesses everyone around you.

DOING AWAY WITH SPIRITUAL FRUSTRATION

We've been talking about natural frustrations that arise on the path to our wild dreams. But what about spiritual frustration? Someone emailed me this question: "Is there such a thing as spiritual frustration? If so, can you explain, and what would you suggest as a solution?" Here's my response:

Yes, I believe there is such a thing as spiritual frustration. You first have to discern if the frustration is a godly or satanic frustration. Sometimes the devil comes with discontent to try to move us out of or ahead of God's will. Other times it's a spiritual frustration from God that moves us further toward His will. Understanding what God's will is and trusting Him to bring it to pass is a key. Much of our spiritual frustration comes from not trusting His timing or not knowing what His will is. Practically speaking, ask God what's causing the frustration, and believe Him for a revelation. Pray in tongues a lot. Confess scriptures over your life that have to do with wisdom and revelation, and watch God expose the root of that spiritual frustration so you can deal with it.

If you are dealing with spiritual frustration, let this prophetic word encourage your heart as you keep pressing into your wild dreams:

> "Remember, you are not the one who causes yourself to grow. For you are growing in My grace. And even though you can't see it with your eyes, know that I've done a deep work, and I'm continuing to do this work in your heart. I am rooting you and grounding you deeply into My kingdom, deeply into My Son. And you might not see the fruit you want to see now, but you will see it. Do not give up and do not grow weary in well doing because in due season—in the *kairos* time, in the perfect moment—you will reap a harvest if you do not faint.
>
> "You will see that peace in your life. You will see that joy in your life. You will see that compassion in your life. I am pulling out weeds that are in your heart even now. I am rooting them out even now, and you will see that as I water your soul with My Word and as you meditate on things I've said to you in past seasons, you are going to

begin to see them manifest," says the Lord, "because you are coming into that place. You have cultivated your heart.

"The fallow ground has been shaken up. You've seen some turbulence in your life. You've seen some things come to the surface, and you said, 'I thought that was gone, Lord. I thought I dealt with that, Lord.' But I have shaken it up," says the Lord, "so it can come to the surface like dross when silver is being refined.

"And you will see, if you are willing to let go—really let go—that I will begin to water what remains and strengthen what remains. Those things that I have put in you, I will strengthen them and bring them to the fore, and people will come to you and say, 'You've changed. What has shifted? What has happened?'

"And you will give Me the glory because you cannot change yourself. But I am changing you. I am the change agent in your life. The Holy Spirit is the change agent in your life—and the Holy Spirit dwells on the inside of you. And He is working on you even when you don't know it. He is whittling away things that don't belong there. And as you yield to Him, as you yield to the work of the Holy Spirit on the inside of you, you will see His fruit manifest, you will see His gifts manifest, you will see the love of God toward others—even those who have wronged you— manifest. You will see it."

Dale Carnegie, an American writer and self-improvement coach, once said, "Our fatigue is often caused not by work, but by worry, frustration and resentment."[3]

DREAM WILD EXERCISES: PRACTICAL STRATEGIES AGAINST FRUSTRATION

Here we talked mostly about the spiritual side of battling frustration. But there are practical, natural strategies you can pursue to alleviate frustration. The first is to figure out what is actually frustrating you. That can be challenging, as you may have more than one frustration—or you may feel overwhelming frustration that's hard to root out. Still, taking some time to determine the root issue is helpful.

Next, think of practical ways to alleviate that frustration. What can you realistically do to alleviate this problem? Is it investing in a new tool? Having a heart-to-heart talk with someone who is not performing duties? Taking some time off to rest? Once you find a solution, act on that solution as quickly as you can so the frustration doesn't linger. Focus on the solution, not the problem, and you won't be so frustrated.

ROOTING OUT EVERY TRACE OF DOUBT

The Holy Spirit is saying, "Doubt is the doorway to unbelief. Doubt is a cousin of fear and suspicion that blocks discernment. The enemy wants you to walk in the curse of doubt. He wants you to worry day and night. But Jesus came to redeem you from the curse of the law. Father has given you the measure of faith that opens the doorway to His promises. Resist doubt as you'd resist the devil, and let your faith rise as you meditate on the blessings I've promised you."

DOUBT IS THE doorway to unbelief." When I heard the Holy Spirit speak those words, I began to ponder the danger of doubt. I understood it was doubt that let the spirit of unbelief erect a stronghold in my soul.

Doubt is uncertainty, but God's Word is certain. Numbers 23:19 assures us, "God is not a man, that He should lie, nor a son of man, that He should repent. Has He spoken, and will He not do it? Or has He spoken, and will He not make it good?" Let God be true, but every man a liar (Rom. 3:4)—and not only every man but every spirit that is not of God. Satan is the Father of lies (John 8:44). He is chief of the fallen angels, including the spirits of doubt and unbelief that are dedicated to carrying out his wicked plots against your wild dreams.

When the Holy Spirit revealed to me that doubt is the doorway to unbelief, I began to see doubt as more than just a mind-set that prevents us from casting the proverbial mountain into the sea. I began to see doubt as a spiritual disease whose goal is to destroy our audacious dreams.

Doubt is a cousin of fear and suspicion that blocks faith and discernment. To doubt is to lack confidence in the Word of God. Doubt is failing to fully trust in the Lord Jesus Christ. Just like alcohol, doubt is a depressant. It damages our heart, lowers our resistance to infection, and leaves us impotent to pursue our godly desires. Just like alcohol, doubt impairs our judgment, brings fatigue, and leaves a nasty hangover all its own. Just like alcoholism, chronic doubt impairs our learning ability, disorients us, and causes mental confusion.

REDEEMED FROM THE CURSE OF THE LAW

In Deuteronomy 28:66 we learn that doubt is part of the curse of the law: "Your life shall hang in doubt before you. You will be in dread day and night and will have no assurance of your life." Thank God that Jesus came to redeem us from the curse of the law (Gal. 3:13). Here's more good news: while alcohol withdrawal can cause tremors and convulsions, withdrawing from doubt causes freedom and liberty in Christ!

In His wisdom God has made it easy for us. He spelled it all out in black, white, and red. Prophets and apostles of old wrote down what He said so we would know His will in all things. We also have chronicles of the lives of faith heroes who stumbled now and again to show us practical lessons for how to avoid the enemy's pitfalls as we pursue our dreams. Modern technology makes it possible to listen to the Word at night while we sleep, look up scriptures on the internet with a few keystrokes, and fly around the world to receive impartations from men and women of God to build our faith and strengthen our inner man.

Here's my point: we have no excuse to doubt or disbelieve His dream for our lives. We can hear the Word through a variety of means. If God had not given us the ingredients to build faith, we could call Him unjust. But He is not unjust. He has given us the ingredients and even told us how to mix them. Faith comes by hearing, and hearing by the Word of God (Rom. 10:17). It's up to us to do our part instead of being like Doubting Thomas, who had to see with his eyes before he would dare to believe (John 20:24–29).

WHAT LENS ARE YOU LOOKING THROUGH?

When my daughter was in elementary school, she was required to take a series of classes known as DARE. The acronym stands for Drug Abuse Resistance Education. She learned the skills she needed to avoid involvement in drugs, gangs, and violence. She learned how to resist peer pressure and live a drug-free life. Part of that training was outlining the danger of drugs and the devastating path drug use takes people down—the path of dream devastation.

It's only appropriate for you to see for yourself in the Word of God how dangerous doubt really is. The Bible has plenty to say about it, and you need to know it so you can fight it off like the demonic power it is. Once you learn to resist doubt, you can receive God's best for your life.

You remember Jesus's sermon about worry? He was talking about natural needs such as clothing and food and drink. In Luke 12:29 Jesus told His disciples not to be "of doubtful mind" (KJV). He also offered some advice for those who were of doubtful mind: seek the kingdom. If you find yourself of doubtful mind, seek the kingdom perspective. It's a command, not a suggestion. Doubting is a sin you don't want to practice because it leads to the death of your dreams. Remember, the Israelites who doubted God died in the wilderness on the way to seeing the dream of entering the Promised Land. God has a better plan for you. But you must believe.

Doubt can also leave you prey to a religious spirit. Remember when Jesus walked in the temple in Solomon's Porch? The Bible tells us that "the Jews surrounded Him and began asking Him, How long are You going to keep us in doubt and suspense? If You are really the Christ (the Messiah), tell us so plainly and openly. Jesus answered them, I have told you so, yet you do not believe Me [you do not trust Me and rely on Me]" (John 10:24–25, AMPC). The Jews took up stones with the intent of murdering Jesus because He told them the truth—and because they doubted what He said.

What about you? Do you believe Jesus, the living Word of God? Do you trust Him and rely on Him and not on your own understanding? Our own understanding often doubts what we don't readily understand. It's easier to believe the reasonable than the impossible, yet Jesus said all things are possible to him who believes—not to him who understands and certainly not to him who doubts. Doubt disqualifies you from the manifested dream.

Here's the problem: we tend to read the Bible through the lens of what we've already been taught or experienced rather than what it truly means. In other words, we often read what we believe rather than believing what we read. If what we read doesn't match what we already believe, doubt finds a crack to seep through. (That's why it's so important who you let feed you spiritual food.) Religion causes us to continually "learn" but never come to the knowledge of the truth. (See 2 Timothy 3:7.) When we doubt that God means exactly what He says He means in His Word, the religious spirit stands ready to lead us into doubt and unbelief. What lens are you looking through? Selah—pause and think on that.

FAITH COMETH, DOUBT KILLETH

Faith comes by hearing. So if you are doubting, you have to ask yourself, What am I hearing? In other words, what are you giving ear to? Are you listening to the still, small voice of God in the matter, or are you listening to the circumstances screaming at your soul? Are you listening to the Holy Spirit or some other spirit? We have to guard our hearts with all diligence because out of it flow the issues of life (Prov. 4:23). Out of our heart also flows the faith that puts the creative force behind our confession. When faith comes, it brings peace, joy, revelation, determination, and other godly manifestations. When doubt comes, it brings fear, confusion, stress, and other ungodly manifestations.

After Jesus was resurrected, some of the disciples were going to a village called Emmaus when Jesus joined them and talked openly with them about the Christ. He called them foolish and slow of heart to believe what the prophets had spoken and what the Scriptures revealed (Luke 24:13–33). These disciples didn't realize it was Jesus until He departed from them, but when they got the revelation that the risen Christ was among them, they returned to

Jerusalem and told the eleven remaining apostles that the Lord had risen. Suddenly Jesus showed up in their midst:

> They were terrified and frightened, and supposed that they saw a spirit. He said to them, "Why are you troubled, and why do doubts arise in your hearts? See My hands and My feet, that it is I Myself. Feel Me and see. For a spirit does not have flesh and bones as you see that I have."
> —LUKE 24:37–39

Can you see how doubt led to fear? The disciples feared because they thought Jesus was an evil spirit, a devil, or some ghost other than the Holy Ghost who had been promised but not yet sent. Kahlil Gibran, a Lebanese writer and artist who lived in the early 1900s, had an interesting perspective on fear. He said this: "Fear of the devil is one way of doubting God."[1] That's a true statement because fear of the devil—or fear of the circumstances he likes to magnify in attempts to cloud the eyes of faith—demonstrates a lack of trust in God's preserving power.

David confronted fear eyeball to eyeball many times. Instead of doubting his God, he spoke the opposite of fear out of his mouth. He spoke faith: "Preserve my life, for I am godly and dedicated; O my God, save Your servant, for I trust in You [leaning and believing on You, committing all and confidently looking to You, without fear or doubt]" (Ps. 86:2, AMPC).

I like this, and it reminds me of a quote attributed to President Abraham Lincoln, the great liberator: "Better to remain silent and be thought a fool than to speak out and remove all doubt."[2] It's better to remain silent and let the devil think you're a fool if you can't offer a faith-filled confession that's pleasing to God. But it's so much better to declare the Word and in doing so build up your faith and remove all doubt about your dreams coming true.

BEYOND THE SHADOW OF A DOUBT

Doubt's ultimate goal is to prevent you from receiving from God—or pursuing His dreams for your life. Doubt causes many people to spend eternity in hell. Doubt even causes many Christians to live below their means, stressed instead of blessed, because they don't have the peace of mind that comes with putting their trust in the living God. Doubt blocks your prayer answers and sets you up to have an evil heart of unbelief that causes you to wander around in the wilderness instead of walking into the promised land.

God is willing to give you the desires of your heart if you are merely willing to believe beyond the shadow of a doubt. Have you ever thought about where that cliché—beyond the shadow of a doubt—came from? If an issue is beyond the very shadow that doubt casts, that means absolutely no doubt remains. It is far enough from doubt that even doubt's shadow does not touch it.

Consider this: the sun and light bulbs give off light. When something blocks that light, it creates a shadow. In light of that truth, consider *Merriam-Webster's* definition of *shadow*: "partial darkness or obscurity within a part of space from which rays from a source of light are cut off by an interposed opaque body; an imperfect and faint representation; an imitation of something; a reflected image; a source of gloom or unhappiness."[3] Doubt's shadow reflects an image all right, but it's the opposite image of truth. It's an imperfect representation of what the Word says. Doubt's shadow casts gloom over our faith and leads us to unhappiness—and unbelief.

There's joy in believing (John 16:24). God's Word is a lamp unto our feet (Ps. 119:105). When the voice of the enemy, negative circumstances, naysayers, or our own impatience in waiting for the prayer answer rise up to block the light of God's truth, we fall prey to the dangers of doubt and ultimately unbelief. I once heard someone say, "Believe your beliefs and not your doubts." Therein lies the key.

DREAM WILD EXERCISE:
ROOTING OUT DOUBT

You can't root out an enemy you can't see. Like any disease, "doubtaholism" doesn't usually kill your belief all at once. Rather, it manifests in progressive stages. The early symptoms are confusion and inaction. Left unchecked, we move on to fear and anxiety. Finally, we continue to instability, double-mindedness, and backtracking that leave us unable to receive the wisdom of God. If you notice any of these symptoms, go to war against doubt. Feed your soul with faith-filled words. Refuse to let doubt derail your dream.

DAY 13

PRUNING IMPATIENCE

The Holy Spirit is saying, "I know patience has never been your strong point. I know it's not fun to wait for Father to move when you can so clearly see the path He has ordained for you. But patience can serve as protection—even a weapon of warfare. Patience will encourage you not to jump out ahead of My leading even when you can clearly see the next step. I see more than the next step and the end goal. I see the obstacles in between that will frustrate your progress if you are not spiritually prepared to overcome them. So be patient. Trust Me. We'll get there."

WHEN I WAS first saved, wise Christians encouraged me to pray fervently for anything according to God's will and He would answer me (1 John 5:14). These same wise Christians warned me never, ever to pray for patience because such petitions would pave the way for trials.

My elders in the Lord based this thesis on James 1:2–3, "My brothers, count it all joy when you fall into diverse temptations, knowing that the trying of your faith develops patience." Indeed, I have learned the hard way not to pray for patience, but I do work to prune impatience out of my life.

The psalmist tells us, "Rest in the LORD, and wait patiently for

Him" (Ps. 37:7). I've learned not to chase my dreams. Instead, I chase the God of my dreams and trust He is faithful to make my dreams come true at the right time. No man on earth and no devil in hell can stop what God wants to do in your life—but you can make a big mess trying to make it happen.

In Genesis 15 God promised Abram and Sarai a son, but they got impatient, and that led to the birth of Ishmael, who brought grief and sorrow into their lives. Manipulating situations may get you somewhere more quickly, but it won't keep you there long. Remember, whatever you do to get somewhere you'll have to keep doing to stay there. You will never have to force anything that's truly meant to be.

After patiently waiting, Abraham obtained his promise, his dream—his son Isaac. It's no different for us. We inherit the promise of God by faith and patience (Heb. 6:15). We must learn to wait for the manifestation of our dreams with patience (Rom. 8:25). Patience also helps cultivate in our hearts the character we need to hold on to the dream when it does manifest (Rom. 5:3–4). Patience is a fruit of the Spirit (Gal. 5:22).

IDENTIFYING IMPATIENCE IN YOUR HEART

Perhaps the best way to identify impatience in your heart is to understand the very definition of *patient*. Merriam-Webster's dictionary defines *patient* as "bearing pains or trials calmly and without complaint; manifesting forbearance under provocation or strain; not hasty or impetuous; steadfast despite opposition, difficulty, or adversity; able or willing to bear."[1]

Because the enemy will adamantly oppose God's dreams for your life, you will surely have to bear pains and trials, manifest forbearance under provocation and strain, and remain steadfast even while you take consistent action toward your dream. Joyce Meyer once said, "Patience is not simply the ability to wait—it's how we behave while we're waiting."[2]

Indeed, our behavior during the process from promise to present reality reveals how much we've matured in the spiritual fruit of patience. Where this spiritual fruit is lacking, you'll see Merriam-Webster's definition of *impatient* rule: "restless or short of temper especially under irritation, delay, or opposition; intolerant; anxious."[3]

Martin Luther, the key figure in the Protestant Reformation, put it this way: "Those speak foolishly who ascribe their anger or their impatience to such as offend them or to tribulation. Tribulation does not make people impatient, but proves that they are impatient. So everyone may learn from tribulation how his heart is constituted."[4]

The fruit of impatience, then, includes: complaining in the face of opposition, reacting when the enemy provokes you, being hasty in decision-making and actions, readiness to give up when you face trouble, getting easily angered at a lack of progress or obstacles, and being anxious or stressed when things don't go as planned. These are all works of the flesh.

The late Watchman Nee, an author and church leader who worked in China in the twentieth century, once said, "Do not be impatient for impatience is of the flesh.... We must distrust the flesh entirely."[5] By contrast, "The fruit of the Spirit is love, joy, peace, patience, gentleness, goodness, faith, meekness, and self-control" (Gal. 5:22–23).

Impatience is the fruit of pride. Patience waits on the Lord. When we don't want to wait on the Lord, we imply that we know better than God when is the best time for our dreams to come to pass. Patience trusts God with the timing. Ecclesiastes 3:1 declares, "To everything there is a season, a time for every purpose under heaven." When we allow impatience to rule in our hearts, we try to change our times and seasons, but Daniel 2:21 makes it clear that this is God's role, explaining that "He removes kings and sets up kings." David rightly told the Lord, "'You are my God.' My times are in Your hand" (Ps. 31:14–15).

OVERCOMING IMPATIENCE

Impatience can delay the manifestation of your dreams because it signals less than total surrender to a faithful God. If you see the fruit of impatience in your life, there is hope. You can overcome this little fox that's spoiling the vine of peace in your life. Here are some tools to help you overcome an impatient soul.

1. Acknowledge your impatience.

The first step to overcoming any problem is moving from denial to acknowledgment. Don't pretend you are not impatient. You aren't fooling anybody around you, and you're certainly not fooling

God. Thankfully He is long-suffering—He is patient—and His grace is sufficient for you to overcome impatience.

2. Repent of impatience.

The Bible tells us that whatever is not of faith is sin (Rom. 14:23). Impatience does not spring from faith; therefore it is sinful. If the fruit of impatience is manifesting in your life, ask God to forgive you for walking by sight instead of by faith.

3. Ask God for grace to wait.

When Paul cried out to God to remove the thorn in his flesh— something he had to patiently endure—God didn't do it. Instead, God told him: "My grace is sufficient for you, for My strength is made perfect in weakness" (2 Cor. 12:9). The Spirit of Grace, the Holy Spirit, lives inside you. He is your helper. Ask Him for help when you feel impatient.

4. Adjust your expectations.

Many times, impatience arises because our expectations of ourselves or others are too high. Years ago the Lord told me to lower my expectations of people, and I would not be so disappointed. If you have high standards, you may find yourself with unreasonable expectations. High standards are excellent, but expectations that exceed God's timing or your own ability will lead to impatience. It's OK to readjust along the way and set more reasonable goals.

5. Discern your triggers.

Like fear or other spiritual issues, impatience can be compartmentalized. You may be excessively patient in some areas and excessively impatient in others. Start paying attention to what triggers your impatience. Is it certain people who push your buttons? Certain situations? When you discern the triggers, you can brace against them so you can respond in a godly manner rather than reacting impatiently.

6. Practice patience.

Move in the opposite spirit. When you feel impatience rising up in your flesh, submit yourself to God, resist the devil provoking you, and crucify your flesh. Make a conscious decision not to get angry, hostile, or anxious.

7. Pray against the emotions of impatience.

Philippians 4:6–7 holds a secret to overcoming impatience. Paul writes: "Be anxious for nothing, but in everything, by prayer and supplication with gratitude, make your requests known to God. And the peace of God, which surpasses all understanding, will protect your hearts and minds through Christ Jesus."

Let me leave you with this quote from Oswald Chambers, an early twentieth-century Baptist and holiness movement evangelist, as he explains "the patience of faith":

> Patience is more than endurance. A saint's life is in the hands of God like a bow and arrow in the hands of an archer. God is aiming at something the saint cannot see, and He stretches and strains, and every now and again the saint says—"I cannot stand any more." God does not heed, He goes on stretching till His purpose is in sight, then He lets fly. Trust yourself in God's hands. For what have you need of patience just now? Maintain your relationship to Jesus Christ by the patience of faith. "Though He slay me, yet will I wait for Him."[6]

Ray Kroc, who built McDonald's into the most successful fast-food chain the world, had a favorite saying: "Press on. Nothing in the world can take the place of persistence. Talent will not; nothing is more common than unsuccessful men with talent. Genius will not; unrewarded genius is almost a proverb. Education will not; the world is full of educated derelicts. Persistence and determination alone are omnipotent."[7]

DREAM WILD EXERCISE: TRADING PEACE FOR IMPATIENCE

We've talked about the spiritual aspects of overcoming impatience, but if you are particularly impatient, you aren't walking in peace. The devil has taken your shoes, and you need those shoes to climb to the mountaintop of dreams realized. I've discovered the so-called serenity prayer is helpful in the face of impatience.

Reinhold Neibuhr penned this prayer many years ago, and it has helped the masses: "God grant me the serenity to accept the things I cannot change; courage to change the things I can; and wisdom to know the difference. Living one day at a time; enjoying one moment at a time; accepting hardships as the pathway to peace; taking, as He did, this sinful world as it is, not as I would have it; trusting that He will make all things right if I surrender to His Will; so that I may be reasonably happy in this life and supremely happy with Him forever and ever in the next. Amen."[8]

SLAMMING THE DOOR ON PROCRASTINATION

The Holy Spirit is saying, "Procrastination is the devil's playground. The longer you put off what I've told you to do, the more leeway you give the enemy of your dreams. The longer you delay taking action by faith in the name of Jesus, the wider you open the door to delay. There is no time like the present; faith is now. Begin to pursue instead of procrastinating one more day. I am with you. I will lead you and guide you. But I need you to take the first step."

JESUS IS THE Alpha and the Omega, the beginning and the end, the author and finisher of our faith. (See Revelation 1:8; 22:13; Hebrews 12:2). Notice that Jesus is the finisher. He always finishes what He starts—and He wants us to finish the God-inspired initiatives we start too. Procrastination has no place in the kingdom—it is an enemy of your wild dreams.

Jesus has given us the keys to the kingdom (Matt. 16:19). Prophetically speaking, the Lord showed me that one of those keys is the "key of finishing." The key of finishing unlocks the blessing of increase and is a clear manifestation of kingship. Of course, you can't finish if procrastination keeps you from starting the race toward your wild dream.

We see in John 5:36 that Jesus had certain works to finish and God was counting on Him to complete them: "I have greater testimony than that of John. The works which the Father has given Me to finish, the very works that I do, bear witness of Me, that the Father has sent Me."

When it comes to finishing, Jesus is our prime example. Jesus was always concerned about finishing the work His Father sent Him to do. He never once let procrastination stop Him. He saw the blessing on the other side of finishing. He had His eyes on the prize—the Father's grand dream to see souls saved—that came after He finished the work of the cross (Heb. 12:2).

Jesus taught His disciples to follow His example and explained the importance of finishing in Luke 14:27–30: "And whoever does not bear his cross and follow Me cannot be My disciple. For who among you, intending to build a tower, does not sit down first and count the cost to see whether he has resources to complete it? Otherwise, perhaps, after he has laid the foundation and is not able to complete it, all who see it will begin to mock him, saying, 'This man began to build and was not able to complete it.'"

Jesus called some to follow Him during His earthly journey to see Father's wild dreams of salvation come to pass, and they procrastinated. Luke gives the account of a man Jesus called who answered, "'Lord, let me first go and bury my father.' Jesus said to him, 'Leave the dead to bury their own dead. But you go and preach the kingdom of God'" (Luke 9:59–60).

This would-be disciple wanted to wait until his father passed away before answering the Father's call. He was procrastinating and missed God's wild dream for his life in that season. Another said, "'Lord, I will follow You, but let me first go bid farewell to those at my house.' Jesus said to him, 'No one who puts his hand to the plow and looks back at things is fit for the kingdom of God'" (Luke 9:61–62).

There are always excuses not to follow God's dream for your life—feeling unworthy, wrestling with fear, not having the resources you need to move forward, persecution from family and friends, and on and on it goes. But when God calls you to move toward your dream, there is grace to press past all resistance available to you. The voice of procrastination will have you put off God's will until you've missed your *kairos* time—your God-given window of opportunity. The good news is there are second chances in Christ. If you've been procrastinating, God wants to help you overcome this tendency right now.

CONFIRMATION BEATS PROCRASTINATION

Before we rush out toward a dream with high emotion, we need to be sure in our hearts the Spirit of God is leading us—and we need to be prepared to pay the price to finish. Both procrastination and failing to finish can lead to unpleasant consequences, even if it's only disappointment in yourself. That disappointment can cause you to lose confidence. Christ Jesus wants us to be confident in His working through us. The other side of the coin is if we aren't utterly convinced God has put His dream in our hearts, the enemy will be able to talk us out of contending to the end. In other words, a lack of confidence in the call flings wide the door to procrastination.

Procrastination can rear its ugly head at any point along the road to your dream realized. You might start out with zeal but begin procrastinating when you dread making a phone call to raise money or completing some task that is difficult for you. You may procrastinate when persecution from friends, family, or demons arises.

No matter the source, never let persecution cause you not to finish a thing. That's just what the devil wants, which is a strong reason he launches an attack. Jesus was persecuted, but He finished anyway. He finished even to the point of death. And when His task was finished, He announced it: "When Jesus had received the sour wine, He said, 'It is finished.' And He bowed His head and gave up His spirit" (John 19:30). Jesus didn't quit, and He didn't procrastinate along the way. And when His mission was complete, He rose to finish His next assignment: sitting at the right hand of the Father, making intercession for us. Praise Jesus!

Think about it for a minute. If Jesus had not finished, then all the stripes He took, all the shame He faced, all the pain He endured would have been for nothing. Without that final act of finishing, the sin of the world would not be atoned for. He had to completely finish the task so that all mankind could be restored to kingship and blessed with eternal life.

Jesus said He who endures to the end shall be saved (Matt. 10:22). He expects us to finish the work God has given us. It brings Him glory when we finish. Yes, we may also have to press through pain to get to the finish line and see our wild dreams come true. When that's the case, we need to keep our eyes on the prize. Ultimately the key of finishing requires Christlike character, specifically endurance, focus, and discipline, which shuns procrastination.

TURNING THE KEY OF FINISHING

Jesus wasn't concerned about food and drink; He was concerned about finishing the work His Father had sent Him to do. John 4:33–34 says, "Therefore the disciples said one to another, 'Has anyone brought Him anything to eat?' Jesus said to them, 'My food is to do the will of Him who sent Me, and to finish His work.'"

Paul knew that bonds and afflictions awaited him, yet he did not procrastinate on his journey. He said, "But none of these things deter me. Nor do I count my life of value to myself, so that I may joyfully finish my course and the ministry which I have received from the Lord Jesus, to testify to the gospel of the grace of God" (Acts 20:24).

In terms of the dreams we pursue, there is rarely any danger to our lives like Jesus or Paul faced, or even many in the persecuted church face today. The only danger, really, is to our "self." Our emotions will help us start pursuing a God-given dream because it's exciting. But our emotions won't carry us through to the end when the work gets hard and the resistance comes. That's when we need discipline, endurance, and focus to battle the temptation to run from persecution.

We're often tempted to put off the next action step toward our wild dreams, even when there is a tremendous financial blessing on the other end. Again, the enemy likes to stop things that are new, and he likes to keep us from finishing. He'll let us wander around in the middle for a while, making some progress, but he doesn't want us to finish because he understands the result of finishing: increase.

Procrastination is a dream killer. Finishing unlocks a blessing. Paul endured. He told Timothy to endure. "So you, my son, be strong in the grace that is in Christ Jesus. Share the things that you have heard from me in the presence of many witnesses with faithful men who will be able to teach others also. Endure hard times as a good soldier of Jesus Christ. No soldier on active duty entangles himself with civilian affairs, that he may please the enlisting officer" (2 Tim. 2:1–4).

Jesus blessed us when He finished the work on the cross. He also got blessed. In fact, He expected a blessing. John 17:4–5 says, "I have glorified You on the earth. I have finished the work You have given Me to do. And now, O Father, glorify Me in Your own presence with the glory which I had with You before the world existed."

We can expect a blessing too—when we finish the work. That blessing is our manifested dreams. Paul told Timothy that he fought a good fight, finished his course, and kept the faith—and we know he received his ultimate dream, to be with Christ: "From now on a crown of righteousness is laid up for me, which the Lord, the righteous Judge, will give me on that Day, and not only to me but also to all who have loved His appearing" (2 Tim. 4:8).

God has dreams of His heart laid up for you. There is a day appointed for your wild dreams to come to pass. Start to see procrastination as the enemy it is, and don't give the devil the satisfaction of persuading you to put off until tomorrow what you need to do today. An old Spanish proverb says, "Tomorrow is often the busiest day of the week."[1]

DREAM WILD EXERCISE:
TAKE ACTION AGAINST PROCRASTINATION

The first step to overcoming procrastination is to recognize this tendency in your life. If you are constantly choosing the easiest things on your to-do list and never getting to more difficult tasks, you are procrastinating. If a certain item stays on your to-do list for weeks, you are procrastinating. If you keep waiting until you feel like doing something on your list, you're procrastinating. Now that you see it, you can search your heart for the reason. Are you afraid? Overwhelmed? Too scattered in your thinking to wrap your head around it? Do you find the task particularly unpleasant? Identify the root cause of the thinking, and then find ways to motivate yourself to take on the task. Set in place rewards, seek an accountability partner, think about the long-term consequences of not following through on the task—and pray.

SENDING PERFECTIONISM PACKING

The Holy Spirit is saying, "No matter how hard you try, you can't live up to everyone's expectations all the time. And if you did, they would just raise the expectation bar higher. Instead of working so hard to please man, focus your strength on pleasing Father. You will never do everything right as long as you are in that fleshly body, but you don't have to be perfect to please the Father. You just have to set your heart to please Him and be quick to repent when you miss the mark. Pleasing God is actually a lot easier than pleasing many people. Indeed, Father will give you grace to press on, and He's much more forgiving than man."

ARTHA, MARTHA, YOU are anxious and troubled about many things" (Luke 10:41). Martha had a servant's heart, but it seems she was a bit of a perfectionist and failed to enjoy the journey with Jesus. Martha welcomed Jesus into her home and ran herself ragged trying to be the perfect hostess. Let's look into the scene:

> She had a sister called Mary, who also sat at Jesus' feet and listened to His teaching. But Martha was distracted with much serving, and she came to Him and said, "Lord,

do You not care that my sister has left me to serve alone? Then tell her to help me." Jesus answered her, "Martha, Martha, you are anxious and troubled about many things. But one thing is needed. And Mary has chosen the good part, which shall not be taken from her."

—LUKE 10:39–42

Jesus might as well have spoken those words to *me*. Maybe you can relate. I often jokingly refer to myself as a recovering perfectionist. If you are anything like me—or Martha—you loathe making mistakes, missing the mark, or otherwise dropping the ball. If you are anything like me, you are too hard on yourself when you do. I've had to learn to stop condemning myself for every little mistake and feeling guilty over everything I didn't do right. I've had to meditate on and embrace, "There is therefore now no condemnation for those who are in Christ Jesus, who walk not according to the flesh, but according to the Spirit" (Rom. 8:1).

It's good to set a high bar for ourselves, but expecting perfection is unrealistic. Even Father God doesn't expect us to think, speak, and behave perfectly. If we could attain perfection on this side of heaven, He would not have sent Jesus to die on a cross. When the Bible says, "Be perfect, even as your Father who is in heaven is perfect" (Matt. 5:48), it means to be complete in Him—not in your flesh. Paul reminds us, "For all have sinned and come short of the glory of God" (Rom. 3:23). Jesus is the only perfect one (1 John 3:5). As we pursue our wild dreams, we have to gaze at the perfect one instead of working hard to make everything perfect. Perfectionism hinders progress.

RECOGNIZING PERFECTIONISTIC TENDENCIES

Before we go any further, let's clearly define *perfectionism*. In this context Merriam-Webster's dictionary defines *perfectionism* as "a disposition to regard anything short of perfection as unacceptable."[1] When you put it in those terms, you can see why the perfectionist—one who subscribes to the doctrine of perfectionism—might never make it to his realized dreams. If you wait for the perfect time to take action, for example, you will probably never take action. Likewise, if you wait for the perfect business partner, you may never start the venture. If you expect everything to be perfect before you launch a product or service, you may never launch it. Ecclesiastes 11:4 warns us: "If you wait for perfect conditions, you will never get anything done" (TLB). Perfectionism is a dream killer because it's a creativity killer. It's an all-or-nothing mind-set that is more likely to get nothing than all. Perfectionism can damage partnerships because you always expect more out of people than what they can give. Perfectionism makes you miserable because nothing is ever good enough. Perfectionism puts you and everyone around you in a pressure cooker. Perfectionism's black-and-white thinking breeds stress, anxiety, catastrophic mind-sets, and overwhelm, and makes it harder to concentrate on the task at hand. So how do you recognize perfectionistic tendencies? Here is a simple self-test for perfectionism:

1. You are on deadline for a project, and it's not up to your standards, so you stay up all night to get it done.

2. When you walk into a room, you immediately notice everything that is out of order, and it bothers you.

3. You procrastinate.

4. When you look at your work—or the work of others—you can't see past the mistakes to the value of the creativity they offered.

5. You get overly upset when things don't work out the way you envisioned them.

6. People flat-out tell you that you are hard to work with or hard to please.

7. Even your best effort is never quite good enough.

8. You are afraid of failure.

9. You get upset when people offer constructive criticism.

10. You get depressed when you don't meet your short-term goals.

If these are consistent behaviors in your life, you may qualify as a card-carrying perfectionist. Jesus made it very clear: "For without Me you can do nothing" (John 15:5). But Paul later reminded us, "I can do all things because of Christ who strengthens me" (Phil. 4:13). If Paul could do all things through Christ who strengthened him, so can we. The question is, Whose strength are we moving in?

In 2 Corinthians 12:9 Paul records a personal prophecy he received: "My grace is sufficient for you, for My strength is made perfect in weakness." Paul's response: "Therefore most gladly I will boast in my weaknesses, that the power of Christ may rest upon me. So I take pleasure in weaknesses, in reproaches, in hardships, in persecutions, and in distresses for Christ's sake. For when I am weak, then I am strong" (2 Cor. 12:9–10).

TEN PRACTICAL STEPS TO OVERCOMING PERFECTIONISM

If you've determined you're a perfectionist, there's hope. You can overcome perfectionism with prayer and practical steps designed to help you set new boundaries for yourself. You can silence your inner critic and find more peace in your heart as you pursue your perfect dreams come true. Here are ten steps to overcoming perfectionism:

1. **Lower your expectations of yourself and others.**
   Many years ago the Holy Spirit told me, "Lower your expectations, and you won't be so disappointed when they aren't met." Perfectionists set a high performance bar—often an unrealistic performance bar. By lowering your expectations to something more reasonable, you can celebrate more wins and record fewer losses. Keep in mind that lowering your expectations—or your standards—does not mean having no standards. Consider that there is a good, perfect, and acceptable will of God (Rom. 12:2). God's will is good, perfect, and acceptable, but in human terms something can be good and acceptable without being perfect—and that's good enough.

2. **Accept your own limitations—and the limitations of the people you work with.** It's been said

team work makes the dream work. We all have limitations. Accept those limitations, and start building a team around you—whether that's friends who can pray strong or have the gift of encouragement or employees who have technical skills necessary to do a job you could never do on your own. We all have different gifts, talents, and limitations. Find your peace with that. We need to take the limits off God but recognize our own limitations. We are but flesh (Ps. 78:39).

3. **Don't major on the minors.** Most people will never see the minor flaws that seem like gaping holes to you. If you hyperfocus on what is wrong, you will never be satisfied with what most people will celebrate. Matthew 7:1 tells us to judge not lest we be judged. We are often harder on ourselves than anyone else—even God. Don't pick yourself or others to death over minor imperfections.

4. **Pursue excellence, not perfection.** There is a difference. Excellence is an impressive standard. Perfection is an impossible standard. Excellence does not demand perfection. Daniel had an excellent spirit in him (Dan. 6:3). The Queen of Sheba marveled at the excellence of Solomon's kingdom (1 Kings 10:4–9). The Bible doesn't say Daniel or Solomon were perfect, but they had an excellence that turns heads. That should be our goal.

5. **Ask yourself, "How important is this, really?"** Yes, there are times to stay up all night to finish a project to perfection. But there comes a point of diminishing return. There comes a time when you can spend another ten hours on something, and it will be only 1 percent better. Understand when enough is enough, and move on to the next goal. Ecclesiastes 2:11 tells us, "Then I turned to all the work that my hands had designed and all the labor

that I had toiled to make; and notice, all of it was vanity and chasing the wind. And there was no benefit under the sun." It's one thing to work hard. It's another thing to toil beyond the point of diminishing return. That, as Solomon said, is vanity.

6. **Don't compare yourself or your work with another standard.** If you do, you'll either be puffed up in pride or feel bad that you or your work aren't measuring up. Paul warned in 2 Corinthians 10:12, "For we dare not count or compare ourselves with those who commend themselves. They who measure themselves by one another and compare themselves with one another are not wise."

7. **Reframe your perspective.** Take a look at the situation from the eyes of another person, and/or ask God to help you reframe your perspective. Also, consider what advice you would give someone else struggling with perfectionistic tendencies—then take it. Things may not be perfect, but God can still use imperfect people and situations to forward your dreams. Romans 8:28 reminds, "We know that all things work together for good to those who love God, to those who are called according to His purpose."

8. **Learn to ask for help.** Ask people to pray for you. Ask people for practical help, feedback, suggestions, and accountability. It requires humility to ask for help, but sometimes you have not because you ask not (James 4:2).

9. **Set proper priorities.** You can't do everything all at once with excellence. This goes back to setting the right goals in the right order. Paul said everything should be done decently and in order (1 Cor. 14:40). That goes for natural as well as spiritual things.

10. **Meditate on God's perfect love for you.** God is
love (1 John 4:8). Think about His love for you,
and let that permeate your perfectionistic mind-set.
You'll stop being so hard on yourself as you receive
a greater revelation of the perfect love that cast out
the fear of not being perfect.

Vince Lombardi offered a healthy perspective when he said,
"Perfection is not attainable, but if we chase perfection we can catch
excellence."[2]

DREAM WILD EXERCISE:
BREAK PERFECTIONISTIC PATTERNS

Perfectionism is a mind-set. You can shake up—and even shock—
that mind-set by taking actions that are purposely imperfect. You
could send an email without spell-checking it, wear a shirt with a
few noticeable wrinkles, or let your dishes sit in the sink all night
after dinner. The point is to make yourself more comfortable with
being less than perfect all the time.

HEART ATTITUDES THAT HELP OR HINDER YOUR WILD DREAMS

*The Holy Spirit is saying, "Attitude is a decision of
our will. You can choose to have a joyful demeanor.
You can choose to walk in peace. You can choose to
maintain a calm heart. You can choose to pursue a
fiery love walk—even with your enemies. You have a
free will. You can make the decision to walk in power,
or you can walk in self-pity. No one can take control
of your attitude—not even Me. So don't blame others
for your outlook, but look up toward Me. When you
feel your attitude deteriorating, start praising Jesus.
Start worshiping Father. Start rejoicing in Me."*

VIKTOR FRANKL AND his wife were deported to the Auschwitz
concentration camp under the Nazi regime in 1944. He
worked for months as a slave laborer before American soldiers
liberated him.[1] Conditions in the concentration camp were hor-
rifying, with contagious diseases spreading rapidly, overcrowding,
swarms of vermin and rats, water shortages, and starvation.

Frankl walked away from this experience with many truths
about the human existence. One of them deals with attitude head-
long: "Everything can be taken from a man but one thing: the last

of the human freedoms—to choose one's attitude in any given set of circumstances, to choose one's own way."[2]

Like Holy Spirit told me, attitude is a decision of your will. This is something Paul the apostle understood long before Frankl walked the earth. Paul was imprisoned more than once. In fact, Paul suffered plenty of adversity as he followed his God-given dreams to preach the gospel to the Gentiles. Paul offered insight in his letter to the church at Corinth:

> ...in labors more abundant, in stripes above measure, in prisons more frequently, in deaths often. Five times I received from the Jews forty lashes minus one. Three times I was beaten with rods; once I was stoned; three times I suffered shipwreck; a night and a day I have been in the deep; in journeys often, in perils of waters, in perils of robbers, in perils by my own countrymen, in perils by the Gentiles, in perils in the city, in perils in the wilderness, in perils in the sea, in perils among false brothers; in weariness and painfulness, in sleeplessness often, in hunger and thirst, in fastings often, and in cold and nakedness.
>
> —2 CORINTHIANS 11:23–27

Paul wrote his letter to the Philippians while standing hip-deep in sewage. He said things such as this: "Only let your conduct be worthy of the gospel of Christ, that whether or not I come and see you, I may hear of your activities, that you are standing fast in one spirit, with one mind, striving together for the faith of the gospel" (Phil. 1:27). In other words, have a good attitude.

Paul said things such as: "Do all things without murmuring and disputing, that you may be blameless and harmless, sons of God, without fault, in the midst of a crooked and perverse generation, in which you shine as lights in the world" (Phil. 2:14–15). In other words, have a good attitude.

Paul said things such as: "Rejoice in the Lord always. Again I will say, rejoice! Let everyone come to know your gentleness. The Lord is at hand. Be anxious for nothing, but in everything, by prayer and supplication with gratitude, make your requests known to God. And the peace of God, which surpasses all understanding, will protect your hearts and minds through Christ Jesus" (Phil. 4:4–7). In other words, have a good attitude.

WHY ATTITUDE IS SO VITAL TO DREAMS COMING TRUE

A positive attitude can help produce positive emotions. According to research conducted by University of North Carolina social psychologist Barbara Fredrickson, positive attitudes fuel feelings of joy, amusement, happiness, peace, and thankfulness, among other emotions. She said in an interview: "I think of positive emotions as nutrients. In the same way that we need to eat a variety of fruits and vegetables to be healthy, we need a variety of positive emotions in our daily experience to help us become more resourceful versions of ourselves."[3]

A bad attitude does not bear good fruit. Bad attitudes will slow you down as you pursue your wild dreams. While there are many bad attitudes that manifest in our lives, these five are some of the most prevalent for wild dreamers. If you discern any of these attitudes in your heart, repent and ask the Lord to help you overcome.

1. **An attitude of complaining:** Complaining may feel good at the moment, but it hinders your wild dreams. I've discovered that complaining about the opposition to my dreams coming true does not move me any closer to my goal. In fact, it wastes time that I could be spending finding a way over the obstacle I'm complaining about. Paul the apostle put it this way: "Do all things without murmuring and disputing, that you may be blameless and harmless, sons of God, without fault, in the midst of a crooked and perverse generation, in which you shine as lights in the world" (Phil. 2:14–15).

2. **An attitude of entitlement:** It seems we live in an age of entitlement, when many people think they deserve success. This attitude breeds laziness. The Bible says, "If any will not work, neither shall he eat" (2 Thess. 3:10). God's dream is His will for you, but that doesn't mean He will deliver it to you on a proverbial silver platter. We can't do God's part, but

God won't do our part. He wants to bless us with the dreams He has inspired in our hearts, but He doesn't owe us anything. Paul tells us, "And whatever you do, do it heartily, as for the Lord and not for men" (Col. 3:23).

3. **An attitude of self-pity:** Anytime self is in the center of your focus, you have the wrong focus—and this focus breeds the wrong attitude. Self-pity is self-centered. When you feel sorry for yourself—when you have a "woe is me" attitude—you are walking in the flesh instead of the Spirit. You are being led by your emotions rather than your God. Self-pity is rooted in pride and can lead to bitterness. Self-pity has no gratitude but only complains. It leads you into a downward spiral into the carnal nature. As you pursue your God-given dreams, you need to pick up your cross and follow Jesus, knowing it might not be easy but it will be worth it. (See Matthew 16:24–26.)

4. **An attitude of blaming others:** It's tempting to blame others when things don't go our way, but this is an attitude that hinders the growth we need to see our dreams manifest. Instead of our taking responsibility for our mistakes, blame points the finger at someone else. When we blame, we fail to change the behavior that caused the mistake. When Adam and Eve were in the garden, they played the blame game rather than accepting responsibility for their actions—and they were cast out of the garden (Gen. 3:12–24).

5. **An attitude of jealousy and envy:** When you are jealous of what someone else has, you are cutting off your channel of blessing and delaying your dream. In fact, you are opening the door to the enemy of your dreams. James 3:16 puts it plainly: "For where there is envying and strife, there is confusion and every evil work."

Just as there are attitudes that stymie your dreams, there are attitudes that set the stage for advancing more rapidly toward your God-given goals. We may have to work to cultivate these attitudes in our hearts, especially if we've embraced a negative bent. But we can renew our minds with the Word of God in these areas as we continue to pursue our dreams.

1. **An attitude of gratitude**: You've heard the phrase "an attitude of gratitude" many times, I'm sure. But are you a doer of this word you've heard? The Bible has plenty to say about thanksgiving. Consider just a few of these verses: 1 Thessalonians 5:18 tells us, "In everything give thanks, for this is the will of God in Christ Jesus concerning you"; Ephesians 5:20 exhorts us to "give thanks always for all things to God the Father in the name of our Lord Jesus Christ"; and Psalm 50:14 says, "Sacrifice a thank offering to God, and pay your vows to the Most High." Giving thanks helps us keep Jesus at the center of our focus.

2. **An attitude of rejoicing**: This is somewhat different from thanksgiving. Rejoicing is having joy in the journey. The Bible tells us to rejoice in our sufferings (Rom. 5:3), to rejoice with those who rejoice (Rom. 12:15), to rejoice and be glad in the day the Lord has made (Ps. 118:24), and to otherwise rejoice always (1 Thess. 5:16). When we rejoice, we are pushing out bad attitudes by focusing our hearts on God.

3. **An attitude of honor**: Honor unlocks rewards. First of all, we need to honor God, but how we treat people also matters to Him. Many people trample over others as they pursue their wild dreams, but honor is God's way forward. Romans 12:10 tells us to prefer one another in honor. We should desire to act honorably in all things (Heb. 13:18). And 1 Peter 2:17 tells us to honor everyone. When we honor others who have gone before us, we can draw

wisdom from their spiritual well. When we honor those around us, we unlock God's favor in our lives.

4. **An attitude of unity:** When we stop striving and competing and seek to unify with those who are laboring in Christ, helping one another reach their dreams, God takes notice and mandates blessings. Psalm 133 spells it out: "Behold, how good and how pleasant it is for brothers to dwell together in unity! It is like precious oil upon the head, that runs down on the beard—even Aaron's beard—and going down to the collar of his garments; as the dew of Hermon, that descends upon the mountains of Zion, for there the LORD has commanded the blessing, even life forever."

5. **An attitude of humility:** Humility paves the way to your dream come true. First Peter 5:6 tells us, "Humble yourselves under the mighty hand of God, that He may exalt you in due time." Alternatively we know pride comes before a fall (Prov. 16:18).

Basketball legend Pat Riley once said, "If you have a positive attitude and constantly strive to give your best effort, eventually you will overcome your immediate problems and find you are ready for greater challenges."[4]

DREAM WILD EXERCISE: DEVELOPING A GODLY ATTITUDE

Developing a godly attitude is a matter of being intentional to discern fleshly attitudes and renew your mind with the Word of God. You will need to pray, meditate on scriptures that tell you the kind of attitude you should have, and maybe ask others around you to make you aware of attitudes you may not see. For example, if pride is manifesting, meditate on scriptures about humility. If fear is manifesting in your attitudes, meditate on scriptures about the love of God because His love casts out all fear. Meditate on the virtuous attitude you want to see manifest, and the Word of God will renew your thinking to line up with God's heart.

LEAVING YOUR COMFORT ZONE

The Holy Spirit is saying, "I am your comfort, yet I will draw you out of your natural comfort zone to encourage spiritual growth. Don't resist My leading, My words of wisdom, or My stretching. I know it doesn't feel good on your flesh—your flesh wars against My Spirit. But I promise you this: if you commit to decrease in your flesh so Jesus can increase in your heart, you will realize greater peace, greater comfort, and greater joy in your life. Will you yield to Me even when it hurts?"

THE HOLY SPIRIT is our Comforter, but that doesn't mean He won't challenge us to leave our so-called comfort zone. Your comfort zone is the place—such as a job, school, people group, or any given situation—where you feel as if you have it all figured out. There's less stress. You're safe. You're in control. You're comfortable.

Most of the time realizing your dreams means stepping outside your comfort zone. Many times seeing your wild dreams come true means allowing God to stretch you beyond your natural limits so you can reach supernatural goals that bring glory to His name. In other words, your Comforter, the Holy Spirit, will often lead you into situations that make you feel ill-equipped, awkward, and stretched like a rubber band while you're dreaming wild.

I speak from experience. I spend several days a week lifting heavy weights and doing all sorts of crazy new exercises in the gym. Sometimes I forget to stretch and end up with muscles so tight I can barely walk two days later. That soreness makes me want to skip the next workout. You might say my muscles are weary in well doing.

When I begin to pursue my God-given dreams, I always wind up in God's gym—lifting heavy spiritual weights and doing all manner of uncomfortable new spiritual exercises that take me far beyond my comfort zone. I don't have to worry about the stretching part. He's doing that too. God's stretching is sometimes as painful on our souls as working over a sore muscle—I'm reminded of Lurch from *The Addams Family* on that medieval-looking stretching machine in the dungeon—but it leaves you with a spiritual capacity great enough to move into the next season He's ordained for you. It forces you out of the comfort zone and into the dream zone.

I'm reminded of the words of Christ recorded in John 15:16: "You did not choose Me, but I chose you, and appointed you, that you should go and bear fruit, and that your fruit should remain, that the Father may give you whatever you ask Him in My name." Jesus could just as well have said, "You did not choose your dreams for your life, but I chose them, and appointed you, that you should go and see your dreams come true." If we truly believe God sees the end from the beginning—and if we truly believe God is the author and perfecter of our faith, our hopes, and our dreams— then we need to trust His leading out of the comfort zone and into the dream zone.

SEPARATING GODLY FROM UNGODLY PRESSURE

One thing I've learned in times of pressure is that there's pressure from the inside—what I call Holy Ghost pressure—and pressure from the outside that comes from people, places, and things (and those "things" include devils). When you step out of your comfort zone, you can be sure the enemy is going to apply pressure to your soul, your flesh, and your tongue. More than anything, he wants you to speak against your wild dreams—he wants you to agree with the vain imaginations that whisper words of defeat to your soul.

We have to discern where the pressure—the stretching—is coming from. It's easy enough to resist God in the name of resisting the devil just because you don't like what's happening and assume the assignment came from the pits of hell. I've seen others lie down and let the devil walk all over them in the name of yielding to the Holy Spirit. Don't do that! Stay prayerful. Ask the Holy Spirit to show you what is of Him and what is against His will for your life. Yield to God; resist the devil. This is not a one-time process. It's an ongoing exercise on the way to seeing your dreams come true.

Here's another thing I've learned about pressure: whether it comes from the hand of God or the enemy, if you'll just keep pressing through the pressure, you'll not only gain strength; the pressure will eventually let up, and you'll find you like your new comfort zone better than your old one. Your new comfort zone is where the next glory is. Your new comfort zone is where your net increase is. Your new comfort zone is where your next dream come true is.

Don't give up when you are between comfort zones—when you are in that desert place between the last glory and the next glory and between the last met goal and the next one. God knows how much you can handle, and He won't let the enemy press you past what you can bear. Through the pressing, you are building spiritual strength and character that will serve you well when you see your dream come to pass. Always remember, sometimes manifesting your victory in spiritual warfare against your wild dreams is merely a matter of outlasting the devil.

Sometimes the pressure comes in the form of pruning. If we won't walk out of our comfort zone toward the dream zone on our own, God will help us. Jesus offers insight in John 15:1–2: "I am the true vine, and My Father is the vinedresser. Every branch in Me that bears no fruit, He takes away. And every branch that bears fruit, He prunes, that it may bear more fruit." Pruning is never comfortable, but when we yield to the divine vinedresser we'll see the fruit of our dreams spring forth in His timing.

FOUR WAYS TO LEAVE YOUR COMFORT ZONE

God has purpose for everything He does. Take confidence knowing that He's stretching you so you can hold more of His power and gain more of His wisdom, more of His character—more of Him. He wants to increase your influence and enlarge your territory. He wants to see His dreams for your life come true, and that often means you need to change as much as or more than circumstances around you need to change.

1. Examine your comfort zone.

Are you content in your current zone? Truly content? If you have a dream that's not realized, the answer must be no. If you are dreaming wild and your dream seems far, far away, how comfortable can you really be? If you have been working the same job with the same pay and the same coworkers for the same ten years, is your faith really being stretched? Life may be easy in your current zone, but easy is the enemy to your dreams. Realizing any dream is a challenge. The good news is you can do all things through Christ who gives you strength (Phil. 4:13).

2. Ask yourself why you won't leave your comfort zone.

Once you've determined your current zone isn't all that comfortable, begin to ask yourself why you continue to dwell there. What lie are you believing? What excuse are you making? What limiting belief have you adopted? What vain imagination are you meditating on? Whom are you trying to please? Whom are you trying not to disappoint? You don't want to look back on your life with regret that you stayed in the comfort zone when the Lord had great plans for your life. Determine the root of the complacency, and war against it.

3. Consider motives for leaving your comfort zone.

What incentive would cause you to step out of the comfort zone into the unknown? What would inspire your heart to take a leap of faith as Abraham did and leave behind the familiar to step into a promise? The answer is your wild dream. Let the desires and dreams God has put in your heart motivate you. Of course, that requires trust. Trusting God means walking by faith and not by sight (2 Cor. 5:7). We can't see God with our natural eyes, but we can discern Holy Spirit's leading and follow Him in childlike faith, knowing that even if we misread Him, He has our backs.

4. Take one step at a time out of your comfort zone.

Some people do drastic things to get out of their comfort zone—quit their jobs, invest all their money in inventions, or move to new cities. If the Lord is leading you to do that, go for it. More often, though, we will walk by faith one step at a time out of our comfort zone. We'll dip our toes in the water and get a taste of freedom and the exhilaration of moving closer to our dreams. That will bring us out of the fear zone and into the faith zone so we can ultimately enter our dream zone.

Let Deuteronomy 1:6–7 speak to your heart even now: "Back at Horeb, GOD, our God, spoke to us: 'You've stayed long enough at this mountain. On your way now. Get moving'" (THE MESSAGE). When you get out of your comfort zone, you'll be more productive, more creative, more energized, more daring, and more able to press toward your dream with everything in you. Get moving.

Richard Branson, founder of the Virgin Group, which has more than four hundred companies under its brand, understands what it's like to press past his comfort zone.[1] He once said: "You don't learn to walk by following the rules. You learn by doing, and falling over."[2]

DREAM WILD EXERCISE: SHAKE UP YOUR COMFORT ZONE

It's been said that insanity is doing the same thing over and over and expecting to get different results. You can make small moves that will help you shake up your comfort zone, such as driving to work on a new road, reading articles and books that challenge your current reality, changing some of your daily routines, taking a pottery class or some other enriching course in your community to meet new people, or volunteering for a local nonprofit. Just do something different.

Part Three

STANDING AGAINST SEVERE STORMS

DAY 18

WEATHERING WILD ADVERSITY

The Holy Spirit is saying, "Be still and know that I am God. The battle belongs to Me. I am your victory banner. I am the captain of the hosts. I am the lifter of your head. I am your defender. I am your vindicator. I am your provider. I will set a table before you in the presence of your adversaries, and they will bow before the Christ in you. You will win if you do not faint. You will gather the spoils if you determine in your heart that you will not withdraw from the battle. You will do this for My glory."

WHEN YOU PURSUE your wild dreams, you'll be met with wild adversity. The good news is you can ride the wind of adversity if you have the right perspective—God's perspective.

See, the devil's adversity coming against you is no match for the God inside you. Greater is He who is in you than he that is trying to kill, steal, and destroy your God-given dreams. (See 1 John 4:4.) The battle in your mind may be raging, but the Lion of the Tribe of Judah inside of you roars louder than the roaring lion that's after you. (See 1 Peter 5:8.)

After I received the dream wild word and started to shift my thinking, I went through eight days of torment—eight days of massive adversity that left me dazed and confused, eight days of spiritual attack that had my head spinning, at least temporarily. It was a sheer blindside from multiple directions.

A psychotic stalker rose up against me. A coven of witches launched a coordinated attack on my life. A Christian woman under the influence of a strong demonic spirit started making moves against my ministry. I experienced major retaliation for standing in the gap for a close friend who was in a major spiritual battle. Misunderstandings and division were manifesting left and right. I had major flu-like symptoms, the likes of which I haven't had in years. My mind was under heavy enemy fire. I could go on, but I'll stop there.

Things lightened up for about a day, and then a new wave of attacks came against me. In total it was four months of massive warfare in almost every area of my life and ministry. There were two choices: let the wind of adversity blow me down, or learn how to ride the wind.

During that time I heard the Lord say: "What the enemy meant for your harm I will turn around for your good as you stay prayerful, stay in My presence, seek My face, and stand in the reality of who you are. Don't let the wicked one move you with the winds and hailstorms. Ride the wind of adversity, and use the storm to your advantage. Rejoice in the tribulation, knowing that your character will become more Christlike as you press into the work of the cross."

THE WAR AGAINST WEARINESS

Adversity to your wild dreams can breed overwhelming weariness. But if perception is reality, then a godly perspective of your trials and tribulations can deliver you from your worst enemy: your own unrenewed mind.

I can't tell you—and, in fact, I'd probably be embarrassed to admit—just how many times I've allowed the perspective of my unrenewed mind to dictate my thoughts, feelings, and emotions in the midst of what I perceived as overwhelming pressure. I can't tell you how many times I didn't think I could take another step; how many times I felt like giving up, calling it quits, throwing in the towel, and moving to some remote tropical island where the devil was less likely to find me.

Then after completely discouraging myself (instead of doing

what David did and encouraging myself in the Lord), I discovered that the pressure isn't as pressing as my perception of reality made it out to be. I was foiled by the enemy that is my unrenewed mind. I took the bait—hook, line, and sinker—by looking at the smoke and mirrors of circumstantial evidence through bleary spiritual battle. (Can I get a witness? Surely, I'm not the only one.)

Of course, later I realize that things weren't really as bad as they looked with my natural eyes. That's why I have asked the Lord over the years to teach me how to quit looking at things through my natural eyes and begin looking at them through eyes empowered by a mind that is set on the things of the Spirit. Paul put it like this: "For those who live according to the flesh set their minds on the things of the flesh, but those who live according to the Spirit, the things of the Spirit. To be carnally minded is death, but to be spiritually minded is life and peace" (Rom. 8:5–6).

See, it's all a matter of renewing your mind to God's perspective. Yes, that means meditating on the Word of God, letting scriptures that deal with areas in which you struggle (whether that's impatience, anger, pride, or some other fruit of a carnal mind-set) roll over in your mind. But I've learned another secret: when we face adversity in pursuit of our dreams, we need to return to the secret place of the Most High. He never faints or is weary—and He can give us the proper perspective on any trial we might be facing. Once we see things from the Creator's perspective, we'll tap into the Creator's joy—and the joy of the Lord is indeed our strength.

A POWERFUL PROPHETIC PROMISE

Here's the promise: "He gives power to the faint, and to those who have no might He increases strength. Even the youths shall faint and be weary, and the young men shall utterly fall, but those who wait upon the Lord shall renew their strength; they shall mount up with wings as eagles, they shall run and not be weary, and they shall walk and not faint" (Isa. 40:29–31).

The renewing of strength is an awesome promise. I'll take the guarantee of not growing weary and fainting too. But I want to point your attention to the other part of this verse: "They shall mount up with wings as eagles." Eagles soar higher than most other birds. Indeed, the eagle is comfortable in high altitudes. The eagle can see at least twice as far as a human.[1] And eagles are symbolic of prophetic ministry.

When you want a prophetic perspective—God's perspective—on anything from your daily trials to your future decisions to the next step toward your wildest dreams in the face of weariness, wait on the Lord. Expect Him. Look for Him. Hope in Him. He will cause you to soar above the storms in your life like an eagle soars above the clouds in the sky. He will give you a prophetic perspective on your situation so you can see the proverbial forest instead of getting overwhelmed by the trees.

Now, it's still up to you to renew your mind to that prophetic perspective. Your unrenewed mind will work overtime to walk you around the same overwhelming mountain once again. After all, that's what the world trained it to do. It's up to you not to be conformed to the world but to be transformed by the renewing of your mind so that you may prove what is that good and acceptable and perfect will of God (Rom. 12:2).

Once your mind is renewed, you'll have that peace that surpasses all understanding—and it will guard your heart and your mind in Christ Jesus. Your perception will still be your reality, but your renewed mind will offer you God's perspective on your wild dreams.

In times of adversity we should take a lesson from eagles. The late Myles Munroe taught me this: "Eagles love the storm. When clouds gather, the eagles get excited. The eagle uses the storm's wind to lift it higher. Once it finds the wind of the storm, the eagle uses the raging storm to lift him above the clouds. This gives the eagle an opportunity to glide and rest its wings. In the meantime, all the other birds hide in the leaves and branches of the trees. We can use the storms of life to rise to greater heights. Achievers relish challenges and use them profitably."[2]

The Word and the Spirit are the wind beneath your wings. When you declare the Word over your life, you can ride the wind. When we wait upon the Lord, we can ride His wind, even in adversity. Winston Churchill once said, "If you're going through hell, keep going."[3] Let's not camp out in the middle of hellish circumstances. Let's keep walking with Jesus to the other side.

DREAM WILD EXERCISE:
RESISTING THE WINDS OF ADVERSITY

In the sudden storms of life we need to know the Word of God—and choose the right weapon for the right battle. Think about it for a minute: Surgeons use different blades for different procedures. Mechanics use different tools to fix different parts of the car. Golfers use different clubs at different areas of the course. Likewise, we need to use the right scripture—the right sword—for the battle. Wage spiritual warfare with healing scriptures if you are sick. Wield financial scriptures if you are facing lack. Swing reconciliation scriptures if you have a prodigal child. Get a concordance or a prayer book if you have to, but in the midst of your trial let your testimony agree with the High Priest of your confession, Jesus (Heb. 3:1, NKJV). Submit yourself to God, resist the devil, and he will flee (James 4:7).

THE WAR AGAINST WEARINESS

The Holy Spirit is saying, "Sometimes you don't fully recognize the level of resistance coming against you because you're so determined to press into My will. I love that about you. Wisdom dictates that when you grow weary, you slow down long enough to discern the assignment against your soul so the enemy's seeds don't take root while you continue plowing ahead.

If you are growing weary, it's a sign that you are either moving outside My grace or moving into enemy territory. Take a moment to ask Me what is going on so you can pull back or press in at the right time."

I F YOU'VE EVER been weary in the midst of walking toward—or walking out—God's dream for your life, you are in good company. Moses grew weary of holding up his hands when the Israelites battled the Amalekites (Exod. 17:11–13). Job grew weary in the midst of his heart-wrenching trial (Job 10:1). And David grew weary of his groaning—he had been soaking his pillow with tears and drenching his couch with weeping (Ps. 6:6). Now that's weary!

What is weariness? Exhausted strength. Failing endurance. Washed-out vigor. Weariness brings with it spirits of heaviness and fainting that make you feel like quitting. Weariness skews your perspective. It causes you to look at the world—and maybe even the church—through bleary eyes. Weariness has friends named Discouragement and Confusion, and together the trio sings a chorus that sounds something like this: "I'm bending over backward, and I'm not getting anything but an aching back. The only light at the end of the tunnel is a locomotive coming to mow me down. Nothing's ever going to change, so I may as well stop trying so hard. I don't even know what I'm supposed to be doing anymore!"

Have you heard that refrain or something similar? It's easy enough to chime in and form a quartet with these voices—or even take the lead. You'll sing your weariness song to anybody and everybody who will listen. Other weary soldiers may join the chorus and even add new lyrics. Remember the old tune "Nobody knows the trouble I've seen. Nobody knows my sorrow"? I think that goes back to Job's days, but many of us still sing that same sad song from time to time.

Look, if you are pursuing God's dream for your life—whether that's heading an international ministry or being the best parent you can possibly be—then you can expect weariness to visit your dwelling place. Over two thousand years ago Jesus pointed out that the harvest is plentiful but the laborers are few. Unfortunately not much has changed in that regard since His days on the earth. When you're pursuing your wild dreams, there usually comes a point when it seems you don't have enough help, time, or energy to press through to the end.

REST IS PART OF THE ANOINTING

So what do you do when weariness comes humming its tune? Well, first fold up your "Super Christian" tights nice and neat, and hang your cape in the closet. In other words, take some rest at the first sign of weariness. Remember, weariness is the first stop on the road to burnout. God commands us to keep a Sabbath day once a week. Even Jesus got tired sometimes, and He is the Son of the living God. Rest is part of the anointing. Just as Rome wasn't conquered in a day, you won't see your dream come true overnight. Pace yourself.

Remember when Jesus and His disciples were on their way from Judea to Galilee? The apostolic gang had to travel through Samaria. Jesus arrived in a town called Sychar near the tract of land Jacob gave to Joseph. Jacob's well was there. "So Jesus, tired as He was from His journey, sat down [to rest] by the well. It was then about the sixth hour (about noon)" (John 4:6, AMPC). Jesus got tired, and it was only noon! So give yourself a break. It's OK to be tired.

Jesus even encouraged His disciples to rest. "And He said to them, [As for you] come away by yourselves to a deserted place, and rest a while—for many were [continually] coming and going, and they had not even leisure enough to eat. And they went away in a boat to a solitary place by themselves" (Mark 6:31–32, AMPC). I can just hear some of you right now saying, "Send that boat my way!"

Now, if you go off in that boat and rest awhile and you are still weary, well, my friends, we've got a different issue. The writer of Hebrews warns us not to grow weary in well doing because we could lose heart and faint in our minds (Heb. 12:3, AMPC). Of course the enemy plans attacks against us while we are weary and weak. (See 2 Samuel 17:1–3.) Again, I believe weariness brings its cousins Discouragement and Confusion, and their melody is as miserable as the saddest country song you'd ever want to hear.

When weariness plagues your mind, it's a signal that your mind is not at rest. You are not resting in the Lord. A perspective change is the prescription for wearing out weariness. Ask the Lord to teach you how to see things through eyes that are set on the Spirit instead of looking at things solely in the natural. As Paul said in Romans 8:5–6, "For those who live according to the flesh set their minds on the things of the flesh, but those who live according to the Spirit, the things of the Spirit. To be carnally minded is death, but to be spiritually minded is life and peace."

WAITING ON THE LORD

Since adversity often brings weariness, we tapped into the prophetic promise of Isaiah 40:29–31 in the last chapter: "He gives power to the faint, and to those who have no might He increases strength. Even the youths shall faint and be weary, and the young men shall utterly fall, but those who wait upon the LORD shall renew their strength; they shall mount up with wings as eagles, they shall run and not be weary, and they shall walk and not faint."

We have a part to play. We have to wait on the Lord. I like how the classic edition of the Amplified Bible expounds on the word *wait* in Isaiah 40:31: "expect, look for, and hope in Him."

When David was in a weary land where there was no water, he earnestly sought God, crying, "My soul thirsts for you; my whole body longs for you" (Ps. 63:1, NLT). He prayed to God, "Strengthen me according to Your word" (Ps. 119:28, NKJV).

If you are weary in running toward your wild dream, Jesus is calling you now to a place of rest in Him. He is saying, "Are you tired? Worn out? Burned out on religion? Come to me. Get away with me, and you'll recover your life. I'll show you how to take a real rest. Walk with me and work with me—watch how I do it. Learn the unforced rhythms of grace. I won't lay anything heavy or ill-fitting on you. Keep company with me, and you'll learn to live freely and lightly" (Matt. 11:28–30, THE MESSAGE).

Unforced rhythms of grace. I like that promise. Let me leave you with one more from Galatians 6:9: "And let us not grow weary in doing good, for in due season we shall reap, if we do not give up." Evangelist Luis Palau put it this way, "When you face the perils of weariness, carelessness, and confusion, don't pray for an easier life. Pray instead to be a stronger man or woman of God."[1]

DREAM WILD EXERCISE: WEARING OUT WEARINESS

Weariness works to wear you out, but you can turn the tables on this enemy of your wild dream by accepting Jesus's promise in Matthew 11:28–30: "Come to Me, all you who labor and are heavy-laden and overburdened, and I will cause you to rest. [I will ease and relieve and refresh your souls.] Take My yoke upon you and learn of Me, for I am gentle (meek) and humble (lowly) in heart, and you will find rest (relief and ease and refreshment and recreation and blessed quiet) for your souls. For My yoke is wholesome (useful, good—not harsh, hard, sharp, or pressing, but comfortable, gracious, and pleasant), and My burden is light and easy to be borne" (AMPC). Don't let the devil burden you with how God will bring your dream to pass with what's in your hand. Ask the Lord to teach you how to enter into His rest, and that weariness will flee.

PRAYING WITH PERSISTENCE

*The Holy Spirit is saying, "You've prayed and
petitioned and offered supplications. You've made
intercession, and you've prayed in the Spirit. This is all
right and in order, but sometimes you need to rise up
and take your authority over a thing. Sometimes after
you've prayed and petitioned and offered supplications
and made intercession and prayed in the Spirit, you
need to decree, declare, and proclaim what you know
is Father's will. Keep decreeing, declaring, and
proclaiming until you see His will come to pass."*

I F FAITH WITHOUT works is dead, then asking without seeking
and knocking is just as lifeless. There are many reasons you may
not be receiving prayer answers on the road to dreams realized—
from doubt in your heart (Mark 11:23–24) to asking with wrong
motives (James 4:3) to unconfessed sin (Isa. 59:1–2) to unforgive-
ness (Mark 11:25) to strife on the home front (1 Pet. 3:7) to turning
away from Scripture (Prov. 28:9).

But you can believe purely, ask with right motives, have a clean
heart, forgive all your enemies, avoid arguments, and soak in the
Word all day and still not see prayers answered. That's because
asking without seeking and knocking flows from the same lazy
river as faith without works.

Before you take offense and stop reading, ponder Jesus's promise on determined, active faith, and then consider two Bible characters' strategies for getting what they wanted. Let's start with Jesus's promise: "Ask and it will be given to you; seek and you will find; knock and it will be opened to you. For everyone who asks receives, and he who seeks finds, and to him who knocks, it will be opened" (Matt. 7:7–8).

Most Bible translators didn't do us any favors with this rendition because it suggests a single request will get the job done. Sure, sometimes a single request suffices. You ask Him. You thank Him for it. And you keep praising Him until you see the prayer answered. But sometimes it takes persistent faith to receive God's promises. Sometimes you have to go after it with godly determination that won't quit until you see your dream come to pass.

KEEP ON ASKING FOR YOUR DREAMS

That's why I like how the classic edition of the Amplified Bible translates Matthew 7:7–8: "Keep on asking and it will be given you; keep on seeking and you will find; keep on knocking [reverently] and [the door] will be opened to you. For everyone who keeps on asking receives; and he who keeps on seeking finds; and to him who keeps on knocking, [the door] will be opened."

This is a promise from God. So long as what you desire is His dream for your heart, you can be assured that if you keep on asking, keep on seeking, and keep on knocking, you will eventually see the dream come true. Let me expound on these three principles:

Ask

Although God knows what we need before we ask Him, He usually won't provide our needs until we ask because He wants relationship with us. So ask, and keep asking until you feel a release in your spirit—and then thank Him until you see the promise manifest. It's also possible that you need to pray more specific prayers. When we pray specific prayers, it helps us clarify what our real need is and heightens our senses when the prayer answer comes. Praying general, blanket prayers is never wrong, but praying prayers specific to your dreams demonstrates an utter dependence on and faith in God. God gives grace to the humble (James 4:6).

Seek

It's not always enough just to ask. More often than not, you also have to seek. Seek the Lord; seek ways to do your part in positioning yourself to receive what you are asking Him for. If you've asked Him for a new job, don't just wait for your dream employer to call you on a random whim. Seek a new job. Fill out applications. Network with people who have influence. Seek what you are after with active pursuit.

If your dream is reconciliation in a relationship, seek reconciliation. If you've asked Him for healing, seek healing. Don't sit back and wait for an angel or your pastor or your friends to do all the work. Faith without works is dead (James 2:26). Now let me balance that before we move on. I started the conversation on seeking with seeking God. That's because you need to be led by the Spirit. You can't bulldoze your way through the doorway to God's dreams for your life. His timing and the will of other people are still at play.

Knock

If you seek, you will find. Once you see God's promise in clear view, knock and keep on knocking until the promised door is open. Knock until your knuckles are sore if you have to. Let's say you've asked Him for a new job. You're seeking a new job and you know in your spirit (or even hope in your heart) that it's a perfect match. Start knocking. God opens doors that no one can shut (Rev. 3:8), but often you have to knock.

Before Jesus's "ask, seek, knock" instruction, He told a parable about a man who wouldn't stop knocking that drives this point home:

> Which of you has a friend and shall go to him at midnight and say to him, "Friend, lend me three loaves, for a friend of mine on his journey has come to me, and I have nothing to set before him"; and he will answer from within, "Do not trouble me; the door is now shut, and my children are with me in bed; I cannot rise and give you anything"? I say to you, though he will not rise and give him anything because he is his friend, yet because of his persistence he will rise and give him as much as he needs.
> —LUKE 11:5–8

SO, HOW DO YOU KNOCK?

In the context of Matthew 7 *knock* means, figuratively, "importunity in dealing with God," according to *Vine's Expository Dictionary of New Testament Words*.[1] That suggests urgent and persistent requests. In other words, once you're sure you've found what you have been asking for—once you see the breakthrough within reach—turn again to asking but with greater urgency.

David sought the Lord in this manner. He declared: "One thing I have asked from the LORD, that will I seek after—for me to dwell in the house of the LORD all the days of my life, to see the beauty of the LORD, and to inquire in His temple" (Ps. 27:4).

David didn't just have a desire; he sought after the object of his godly desire. He had persistent faith. If you read the Psalms, pursuing God was a constant theme in his writing. Looking at our three-step process, David desired (ask) and sought (seek). Based on David's relationship with the Lord, which we read about in the Word, I believe he found what he asked for, then inquired (knock). God opened the door to intimacy.

Much the same, consider the parable of the persistent widow. Jesus used the parable to teach us that we should always pray and not lose heart. Jesus also showed us that the widow did more than ask—she kept on asking, kept on seeking, and kept on knocking. Read the parable, and see this with your own eyes:

> He said: "In a city there was a judge who did not fear God or regard man. And a widow was in that city. She came to him, saying, 'Avenge me against my adversary.'
>
> "He would not for a while. Yet afterward he said to himself, 'Though I do not fear God or respect man, yet because this widow troubles me, I will avenge her, lest by her continual coming she will weary me.'"
>
> And the Lord said, "Hear what the unjust judge says. And shall not God avenge His own elect and be patient with them, who cry day and night to Him? I tell you, He will avenge them speedily. Nevertheless, when the Son of Man comes, will He find faith on the earth?"
>
> —LUKE 18:2–8

George Mueller, a nineteenth-century Christian evangelist known for building orphanages, once said: "It is not enough to begin to pray, nor to pray aright; nor is it enough to continue for a time to pray; but we must pray patiently, believing, continue in prayer until we obtain an answer."[2]

PRAY ONCE OR KEEP PRAYING?

Can you see it? There is a time to pray once, hand it over to God, and trust Him to answer. But there is also a principle of persistent faith that says you ask and keep on asking, seek and keep on seeking, and knock and keep on knocking until you receive the promise. How do you know the difference? The easy answer is to be led by the Spirit.

A deeper answer is to consider the opposition. When you face opposition to walking through the doorway of your dreams, ask God to show you what to do to position yourself for the manifestation, and then take any God-inspired action (seek) to find the doorway He leads you to. Once you find the door, start knocking and keep knocking. God will surely open it at the appointed time.

DREAM WILD EXERCISE: RELEASING PRAYER POWER

James 5:16 assures us, "The earnest (heartfelt, continued) prayer of a righteous man makes tremendous power available [dynamic in its working]" (AMPC). It's not enough to say rote prayers out of obligation. Robotic prayers lack the fervency that touches God's heart. Although God hears any prayer according to His will, releasing tremendous, dynamic power demands not only continual prayer but earnest, fervent, heartfelt prayer. Cry out to God as if you are desperate for your wild dreams to come to pass. He hears desperate prayers. Read 1 Samuel 1:1–15, and let these verses encourage your heart.

THE BATTLE FOR FOCUS

*The Holy Spirit is saying, "When you face an obstacle
of any kind, you have two clear choices: focus on
the obstacle and get frustrated with the one you
believe put it there, or focus on the solution and the
One who has the wisdom to help you overcome the
obstacle. There will always be obstacles, and if you
focus too much on them, you'll become discouraged.
See the obstacles—but then turn to the One who
has the wisdom and strategy that will lead you
into victory. Only you control what you focus on."*

W E ALMOST ALWAYS hit the skids at some point on the fast
track to our wild dreams. When we do, we should take a
lesson from NASCAR drivers. These daredevils race at
speeds in excess of two hundred miles per hour, leaving little room
for error. If you've watched NASCAR races, though, time and time
again you see drivers crash into the wall and go up in flames, often
taking out other racers with them.

What happened? Any number of dangers can emerge on the
racetrack. Sometimes drivers clip the backs of cars in front of them
because they were going a little too fast. (Be careful not to get
ahead of God!) Other times they misjudge a turn. (Listen carefully to His voice!) Many times those mistakes send the race car

drivers heading full-speed into the retaining wall, and serious injuries, even death, occur.

When their cars spin out of control, race car drivers are trained to focus on where they want the cars to go rather than where the cars are headed. They are schooled to pull the wheel in the opposite direction of the wall that could put an end to their dream of winning the race.[1]

Here's the principle: you will always move toward what you focus on. When you feel as if you are spinning out of control—when you feel as if you are about to hit a wall—you have two choices. You can focus on the problem, or you can focus on the solution. You can keep heading toward a crash, or you can pull out of the tailspin by refocusing your mind on Jesus.

As you run your race toward your wild dream, you'll have to fight the good fight of faith to focus. The enemy will war against your mind to win your focus. Winning the battle for focus will expedite your journey on the road to realized dreams.

RUNNING TOWARD YOUR DREAM WITH FOCUS

Paul the apostle put it this way: "Do you not know that all those who run in a race run, but one receives the prize? So run, that you may obtain it. Everyone who strives for the prize exercises self-control in all things" (1 Cor. 9:24–25). You could just as easily say: "Everyone who presses toward his dream needs to exercise self-control in the area of focus."

Paul understood that what you focus on grows. You've heard the idiom "He made a mountain out of a molehill." That essentially means someone is making a big deal out of a minor issue. That happens when we focus on the problem instead of the solution. It happens when the enemy pulls our focus from our wild dreams to his smoke and mirrors that magnify his schemes over the Lord's dreams. Focus is a key to seeing dreams come true.

Paul was also clear that he did not run with uncertainty (1 Cor. 9:26). The New Living Translation describes his run as "with purpose in every step," and the International Standard Version says he ran "with a clear goal in mind." Paul was focused on the dream God put in his heart. He could have hyper-focused on his persecutors, the thorn in his flesh, the beast at Ephesus, or one of many other trials. He mentioned these things as teaching tools, but his focus was always on finishing his race.

Paul won the battle for focus. He shared his victory with his spiritual son, Timothy: "I have fought a good fight, I have finished my course, and I have kept the faith. From now on a crown of righteousness is laid up for me, which the Lord, the righteous Judge, will give me on that Day, and not only to me but also to all who have loved His appearing" (2 Tim. 4:7–8).

Paul's ultimate dream came true, which was to be with Jesus. No devil can stop you from seeing that eternal dream become a reality, but God has a dream for you on this side of heaven. He has a purpose, a plan, and a goal for you to reach. There is a good fight of focus to win for His glory.

SIX TACTICS TO HELP YOU STAY FOCUSED

In elementary school we learn reading, writing, and arithmetic. We are taught to sit up straight and pay attention. But most of us were never taught how to focus. Distractions abound, but if you can learn to focus, you can demolish these devilish agendas to delay your wild dreams. The late Zig Ziglar, an author and motivational speaker, once said, "Lack of direction, not lack of time, is the problem. We all have twenty-four-hour days."[2] Indeed, that's why Paul cautioned us to make the most of our time because the days are evil (Eph. 5:16). Here are six strategies to stay focused amid mass distractions.

1. Eliminate every possible distraction.

Some distractions are especially obvious. Your smartphone dinging every five minutes is an obvious distraction. Constantly checking email, social media, and other technology platforms can distract you from focusing on the top three goals you need to achieve each day to keep steady progress toward your dreams. Barking dogs, crying kids, and visits from coworkers can distract you. Put your phone in the other room. Shut down your email. Decide not to use social media until after work. Put a "Do not disturb" sign on your door. Bruce Lee once said, "The successful warrior is the average man with laser-like focus."[3]

2. Avoid too much multitasking.

I'm the ultimate multitasker. While a slow webpage is loading, I'll check my email. While I'm on hold with customer service, I'll brew some coffee. I want to keep the momentum strong, but too much multitasking can introduce distractions and lower your productivity. Use wisdom in multitasking. Alexander Graham Bell put it this way: "Concentrate all your thoughts upon the work at hand. The sun's rays do not burn until brought to a focus."[4]

3. Stop chasing bright, shiny objects.

As you pursue your wild dreams, you'll be tempted to veer off onto rabbit trails and chase bright, shiny objects that are alluring. It may seem like an avenue you need to pursue, a relationship you need to forge, or some other activity that would help you. But if it's not part of the vision or action plan—or if you don't have a leading from the Lord to take the rabbit trail—stop and refocus on the big picture. God sometimes will lead you down a rabbit trail to find a divine connection, but the enemy often puts bright, shiny objects in your path to distract you. Bill Gates, cofounder of Microsoft, is quoted as saying, "My success, part of it certainly, is that I have focused in on a few things."[5]

4. Prune non-fruit-bearing activities.

There's a difference between business and fruitfulness. You can stay busy all day long with activities that don't move you toward your goal. If you are noticing you work hard all day and are not moving toward goals that lead you to your dreams, examine the fruit of your labors. Delegate what you can delegate, and prune what needs to be pruned so you can bear more fruit. Poet Ralph Waldo Emerson is often quoted as saying, "As the gardener, by severe pruning, forces the sap of the tree into one or two vigorous limbs, so should you stop off your miscellaneous activity and concentrate your force on one or a few points."[6]

5. Don't overcomplicate things.

You've probably heard the phrase "Keep it simple, silly." Well, that's not exactly how the saying goes, but you know what I mean. The enemy works to overcomplicate things. When things get complicated, break down the task or the situation into simple steps that bring you toward a solution. Keep your thinking simple. Steve Jobs, cofounder of Apple, shared: "That's been one of my mantras—focus and simplicity. Simple can be harder than complex: you have to work hard to get your thinking clean to make it simple. But it's worth it in the end because once you get there, you can move mountains."[7]

6. Practice concentration skills.

Focus and concentration go hand-in-hand. If you can concentrate on your key focus, you can move more rapidly toward your wild dreams. Concentration is a short-term skill demanded for long-term focus.

You practice concentration skills by first deciding what you want to concentrate on and fighting off every thought or temptation to concentrate on something else. Thoughts about random tasks will pop up in your mind as you try to concentrate, much the same as when you try to pray or read the Word. Write those thoughts down to get them off your mind, and then keep concentrating on the task at hand.

As Zig Ziglar once said, "I don't care how much power, brilliance or energy you have, if you don't harness it and focus it on a specific target, and hold it there you're never going to accomplish as much as your ability warrants."[8]

DREAM WILD EXERCISE:
TRACK YOUR TASKS

Write down every little thing you do and how much time you spend doing it for an entire workweek. This may seem like a mundane activity—and maybe even overwhelming—but if you oblige me, you'll quickly discover where you are really focusing your time. This exercise is akin to looking at your bank account ledger. Just as your ledger or credit card statement shows you where you are spending your money, this sheet will show you how you are spending your time.

Look for time stealers, mass distractions, and low-value activities that are dominating your days. You may have to do this exercise more than once to get the full effect, especially if your weekly activities vary. You can also use apps such as RescueTime online to help you track your time efficiently.[9]

DAY 22

ASK GOD TO PUT HIS DESIRES IN YOUR HEART

The Holy Spirit is saying, "I am the One who put My dream in your heart. I am the One who gave you the desire to heal the sick. I am the One who draws you to the secret place to cry out for the dreams and desires I have put in your heart. So continue drawing near to Me, and I will continue drawing near to you. I will help you manifest your purpose and walk in your destiny. I will show you what to let go of and what to grab hold of. I will help you align your will perfectly to Mine and release My gifts in faith."

W HEN I FIRST got saved, a young man I knew was head over heels in love with a friend of mine. He would do anything for her, but she just toyed with him shamelessly. It was difficult to watch. The young man sought counsel from an elderly woman in the church on how to catch his dream girl. Her advice was straight out of Psalm 37:4: "Delight yourself in the LORD, and He will give you the desires of your heart."

The young man walked away determined to delight himself in the Lord, convinced God would give him the desire of his heart—his dream girl. After he walked off, the elderly woman filled me in on the part she didn't tell him. She shared, "When he delights himself in the Lord, God will give him a new dream of his heart because that girl is not for him. He is so focused on this girl he is missing God's greater will for his life."

That day I learned a lesson. Every human being on the planet has dreams, ambitions, and aspirations, but at least some of them likely spring from the lust of the flesh, the lust of the eyes, or the pride of life. (See 1 John 2:16.) Pursuing carnal lusts out of egotism won't ultimately satisfy your soul.

We've talked about demonic opposition to our wild dreams, from vain imaginations to sudden storms. But have you ever considered that you are also in a spiritual war against your own carnal lusts? When Paul said we don't wrestle against flesh and blood (Eph. 6:12), he did not mean that we don't wrestle against fleshly temptations. Indeed, we know that carnal lusts war against our soul (1 Pet. 2:11). We have to engage in this battle in order to walk out our destiny in Christ.

If we want God's wild dreams for our lives, we need to cry out to Him and wage war on carnal lusts that rise up to defy His counsel. After all, Proverbs 19:21 tells us, "There are many plans in a man's heart, nevertheless the counsel of the LORD will stand."

When we leave God's counsel out of our dreams, we enter into presumption and could end up with devastation instead of His perfect will for our lives. James warns: "Come now, you who say, 'Today or tomorrow we will go into this city, spend a year there, buy and sell, and make a profit,' whereas you do not know what will happen tomorrow. What is your life? It is just a vapor that appears for a little while and then vanishes away. Instead you ought to say, 'If the Lord wills, we shall live and do this or that.' But now you are rejoicing in your boastings. All such rejoicing is evil" (James 4:13–16).

Because our flesh is not completely crucified—our flesh wars against the Spirit, and the Spirit wars against our flesh (Gal. 5:17)—we are wise to ask God to put His desires in our hearts and stand strong against any demonic or fleshly counsel.

RECOGNIZING CARNAL LUSTS

Vine's Expository Dictionary of New Testament Words defines *lust* as a "strong desire of any kind."[1] Although the Bible uses *lust* in a positive context three times, the Word of God most often describes it as a root of sin. Lust is associated with pride, greed, and other strong desires that lead us out of God's will. James 1:13–15 tells us, "Let no man say when he is tempted, 'I am tempted by God,' for God cannot be tempted with evil; neither does He tempt anyone. But each man is tempted when he is drawn away by his own lust and enticed. Then, when lust has conceived, it brings forth sin; and when sin is finished, it brings forth death."

We must wage war on carnal lusts because these strong desires ultimately bring forth death instead of dreams in our lives. Paul understood this all too well. Paul not only wrestled the beast at Ephesus (1 Cor. 15:32); he also wrestled his own carnal desires. He shared his heart in the Book of Romans. He knew the right thing to do, but the power of sin kept sabotaging his best intentions. He had a will to do what is right but an inability to follow through. He would decide not to do bad then do bad anyway. Sound familiar? Take a look at Paul's confession:

> Something has gone wrong deep within me and gets the better of me every time. It happens so regularly that it's predictable. The moment I decide to do good, sin is there to trip me up. I truly delight in God's commands, but it's pretty obvious that not all of me joins in that delight. Parts of me covertly rebel, and just when I least expect it, they take charge. I've tried everything and nothing helps. I'm at the end of my rope. Is there no one who can do anything for me? Isn't that the real question?
> —ROMANS 7:20–24, THE MESSAGE

That is the real question. But thanks be to God, who always causes us to triumph in Christ (2 Cor. 2:14). Jesus Christ acted to set things right in a life of contradictions where Paul wanted to serve God with all his heart and mind but was pulled by his carnal nature to do something that would delay God's dream for his life. Christ is our secret weapon in the war against carnal lusts too. Paul won the war against his soul—and he showed us how to win too.

When carnal desires come knocking on the door of your mind, when selfish ambition wants to lead you off God's perfect path, don't ignore them. Confront them with the weapons of your warfare, which are not carnal but mighty in God for pulling down strongholds (2 Cor. 10:4). Take those thoughts captive, and dream with God instead.

DISCERNING GOD'S DREAM FOR YOUR LIFE

After you've rooted out carnal lusts and asked God to put His desires in your heart, you may still struggle to determine God's specific dream for your life. Although God delights in your prayers (Prov. 15:8) and promises to give you the desires of your heart when you delight yourself in Him (Ps. 37:4), it can take time to discern God's dream for your life in any given season. Consider the following to help you discern God's dream for your life.

Don't try to figure it out in your head.

Instead of trying to figure things out, ask the Lord and trust Him to open your eyes. We read in Proverbs 3:5–6: "Trust in the LORD with all your heart, and lean not on your own understanding; in all your ways acknowledge Him, and He will direct your paths." God will direct your path toward your dreams when you get out of your head and press in to His heart.

Surrender your will to Him fully.

Ultimately we need to surrender to God because sometimes the desires He puts in our hearts seem contrary to our own desires. As we surrender to His will, His desires become our desires. When we live a sacrificial life of service to Him, our minds become renewed to His plan. Romans 12:1–2 tells us, "I urge you therefore, brothers, by the mercies of God, that you present your bodies as a living sacrifice, holy, and acceptable to God, which is your reasonable service of worship. Do not be conformed to this world, but be transformed by the renewing of your mind, that you may prove what is the good and acceptable and perfect will of God."

Take note of your natural gifts and passions.

The passion of your heart, along with your gift mix, will give you some clue about God's dream for your life. (See 1 Peter 4:10.) Although you may need to develop skill sets to pursue your wild dreams, you will have a passion and zeal to do the work it takes to drive you toward your godly desires. You can even ask others

what gifts they see operating in your life. (See Proverbs 11:14.) Rick
Warren, best-selling author of *The Purpose-Driven Life*, explains,
"God's dream for your life is exponentially bigger than your dream.
It's eternally significant."[2]

DREAM WILD EXERCISE: WALKING OUT PSALM 37:4

Psalm 37:4 promises us that if we delight ourselves in the Lord,
He will give us the desires of our hearts. How do we practically
walk in Psalm 37:4? How do we delight ourselves in the Lord?
When we delight ourselves in the Lord, we're taking delight in
who He is, His Word, and His instructions, and living a life that
thrills His heart. The Hebrew word for delight in this verse can
be translated "to be happy about, take exquisite delight."[3] And
Merriam-Webster defines *delight* as "a high degree of gratification
or pleasure; extreme satisfaction."[4]

Two verses may help you understand this further. The psalmist
says, "I delight to do Your will, O my God; Your law is within my
inward parts" (Ps. 40:8). And Paul wrote, "For I delight in the law
of God according to the inner man" (Rom. 7:22). Seek to walk in
God's will, to obey His commands, and to walk in His ways, and
you won't miss His dream for your life. And don't pressure yourself to be perfect. Remember, perfectionism is a dream killer. No
one is perfect, but we can seek perfect obedience and repent when
we blow it.

Part Four

RUNNING THE RACE TOWARD YOUR DREAMS

DAY 23

IMAGINE WHAT YOU WOULD DO WITH LIMITLESS MONEY

The Holy Spirit is saying, "When the enemy messes
with your finances, it can strike fear in your soul.
When you take that financial hit, it can bring worry
and doubt and a flood of emotions to your mind.
Remember, the lilies do not toil, nor do they spin, yet
they are clothed. The birds do not sow or reap or store
food, but they are fed. Don't worry about what you will
eat or drink or what clothes you put on. Father will not
leave you without the things you need. He will not."

IMAGINE FOR A moment that money were not an issue. What would you do? Now, what if I told you money is not an issue? Lack is a lie of the enemy. When God puts His dream in your heart, He will pour out the resources you need as you need them to make even your wildest dreams come true. The devil may resist that outpouring—you may have to contend in the spirit to receive the provision you need—but your faith will pull from heaven the necessary funds to drive your dream toward reality.

So again, take a moment to imagine what you would do if money were not an issue. How would that change your perspective on your God-given dreams? The devil wants us to serve mammon—to be enslaved to currency. The devil wants us to carry a poverty mind-set. The devil wants us to look at financial challenges through the eyes of the world instead of through the eyes of God. Many of us are unknowingly serving mammon and looking to our employer as the source of our income instead of the God who created all things.

Jesus taught us, "No one can serve two masters. For either he will hate the one and love the other, or else he will hold to the one and despise the other. You cannot serve God and money" (Matt. 6:24). The Amplified Bible, Classic Edition really draws it out: "No one can serve two masters; for either he will hate the one and love the other, or he will stand by and be devoted to the one and despise and be against the other. You cannot serve God and mammon (deceitful riches, money, possessions, or whatever is trusted in)." And The Message Bible reads, "You can't worship two gods at once. Loving one god, you'll end up hating the other. Adoration of one feeds contempt for the other. You can't worship God and Money both."

When we trust in money to carry us toward our wild dreams, we're in danger of serving the wrong god, tapping into the wrong spiritual principles, and otherwise building on a foundation that will crumble when the storms come. On the other hand, when we trust in God to carry us toward our wild dreams, our assurance is based on biblical principles, and we are building on a foundation of faith that will stand against any demonic windstorm. When we serve God, there is no limit to the resources He can pour out from the windows of heaven—blessings we can't contain. (See Malachi 3:10.)

GOD OWNS EVERYTHING IN THE UNIVERSE

God owns the cattle on a thousand hills (Ps. 50:10). The silver is His, and the gold is His (Hag. 2:8). The seas and the mountains are His (Ps. 95:5). The earth is full of His possessions (Ps. 104:24). As the psalmist writes, "The earth belongs to the LORD, and its fullness, the world, and those who dwell in it" (Ps. 24:1).

Are you getting the picture? God owns everything. If He gave you a dream, He can pull from vast resources to help you bring it to pass. Of course we receive from Him by faith, and the enemy battles against our minds with vain imaginations that defy the Word of God in our lives. The devil wants to turn your dream into a nightmare, and he's strategic in his competitive campaign against God's will for you by making it all about the money, or lack of money.

In the corporate world they call this a FUD campaign. FUD is an acronym for fear, uncertainty, and doubt. Essentially it's a disinformation strategy. Wikipedia explains that "FUD is generally a strategy to influence perception by disseminating negative and dubious or false information and a manifestation of the appeal to fear."[1] FUD is propaganda. Some claim an IBM exec created this terminology, but Satan was using it far before modern technology wars entered the scene.

If the enemy can get you to doubt God's provision in your life, he can effectively steal, kill, and destroy your dream. John 10:10 tells us the enemy's strategy is to kill, steal, and destroy, but Jesus said He came that we "may have and enjoy life, and have it in abundance (to the full, till it overflows)" (AMPC). God is a God of abundance. The psalmist assures us, "I have been young, and now am old; yet I have not seen the righteous forsaken, nor their offspring begging bread" (Ps. 37:25).

John the apostle wrote, "Beloved, I wish above all things that thou mayest prosper and be in health, even as thy soul prospereth" (3 John 1:2, KJV). Your soul will prosper when you renew your mind with the Word of God about His provision for you.

YOU HAVE THE POWER TO CREATE WEALTH

Keep imagining what you could do with limitless money. Now understand the reality of Deuteronomy 8:18: "But thou shalt remember the LORD thy God: for it is he that giveth thee power to get wealth, that he may establish his covenant which he sware unto thy fathers, as it is this day" (KJV).

The Hebrew word for "power" in that verse is often translated to mean "strength, power, and might,"[2] and "get wealth" means "to accomplish wealth, produce wealth, make wealth."[3] When you have wealth, you have an abundant supply, and you are living on the right side of John 10:10 and are positioned to glorify God. Poverty does not glorify God.

I used to have a poverty mind-set. I lost everything I had shortly after my husband abandoned me and left me with our then two-year-old daughter. I was on food stamps and stockpiled food. I would consume things sparingly. I would even let my foot off the accelerator on my car to save gas going down a hill. I was stressed about money. See, I didn't understand Matthew 6:28–33:

> Why take thought about clothing? Consider the lilies of the field, how they grow: They neither work, nor do they spin. Yet I say to you that even Solomon in all his glory was not dressed like one of these. Therefore, if God so clothes the grass of the field, which today is here and tomorrow is thrown into the oven, will He not much more clothe you, O you of little faith? Therefore, take no thought, saying, "What shall we eat?" or "What shall we drink?" or "What shall we wear?" (For the Gentiles seek after all these things.) For your heavenly Father knows that you have need of all these things. But seek first the kingdom of God and His righteousness, and all these things shall be given to you.

I'll never forget the day when the revelation of this passage hit me. I picked up my daughter from nursery school, and I was especially stressed out about money that day. I didn't know how I was going to pay my bills. This was particularly uncomfortable for me because I had always had money. As I strapped Bridgette into her car seat, she said, "Mommy, I have something to tell you." She proceeded to prophesy Philippians 4:19 to me, "My God shall supply your every need according to His riches in glory by Christ Jesus." That opened my eyes, and my eyes have stayed open ever since.

PRINCIPLES OF SOWING AND REAPING

I've learned that what I make happen for someone else, God will make happen for me. The key is to let the Lord lead you in your sowing and doing everything as unto the Lord. Ephesians 6:5–8 confirms this:

> Servants, obey those who are your masters according to the flesh, with fear and trembling, in sincerity of your heart, as to Christ, not serving when eyes are on you, but as pleasing men as the servants of Christ, doing the will of God from the heart, with good will doing service, as to

the Lord, and not to men, knowing that whatever good thing any man does, he will receive the same from the Lord, whether he is enslaved or free.

When I set out to pursue a new God-given dream, I set my heart to sow into the lives of those who have achieved a similar dream. You can sow your prayers, your time, or your money. I do all three, but sowing your finances into someone else's dream is, in my experience, the fastest way to unlock provision for your own dream. Galatians 6:7 tells us, "For whatever a man sows, that will he also reap." The good news is the law of the harvest reveals you always reap more than you sow. As you seek finances to fund your dream, ask, seek, knock—and sow.

Minister and author Norman Vincent Peale said, "Empty pockets never held anyone back. Only empty heads and empty hearts can do that."[4]

DREAM WILD EXERCISE: MEDITATE ON PROVISION SCRIPTURES

Jesus talked more about money than about any other single issue— including heaven or hell. Jesus spoke of money in sixteen of the thirty-eight parables He offered in the New Testament. Understand what Jesus said about money, and then meditate on scriptures about God's provision for you. Here's a list of verses to get you started: Psalm 23:1; 37:25; Matthew 6:26, 33; Romans 8:32; 2 Corinthians 9:8; and Philippians 4:19.

WHAT IF YOU COULD NOT FAIL?

*The Holy Spirit is saying, "Anything is possible. All
things are possible. Nothing is impossible. Act as if
you believe that. Take risks that seem unusual. Stretch
beyond the limitations of your mind, and dream big,
pray in faith, intercede with confidence, stretch out
your hands, and ask for the healing anointing to
flow. All things are possible to the one who believes. I
have put My gifts within you. The Spirit that raised
Christ from the dead dwells on the inside of you. I am
praying with you. You cannot fail if you follow My
lead. So listen to My voice, believe I am speaking, step
out in faith, take a risk, and watch miracles happen."*

WHAT WOULD YOU do if you could not fail? If you were absolutely guaranteed success in your venture, how would that change your thoughts, words, and deeds right now? Would the impossibility of failure inspire greater faith in your heart, like what David had when he ran to the battle line to defeat Goliath? Would knowing you could not lose make you strong and courageous, as Joshua was when God charged him with entering the Promised Land? Would guaranteed success make you more willing to sacrifice your temporary comfort for your dream, as Christ did on the cross?

I ask you again, what would you do if you could not fail? I have good news for you: you cannot fail in Christ. Jehovah Nissi, which means "the Lord is my banner," assures your victory when you follow His dream for your life. First Corinthians 15:57 promises, "But thanks be to God, who gives us the victory through our Lord Jesus Christ!" You might fail to hit specific goals or meet various deadlines, but if you don't quit, you'll win in the end. You are unstoppable in Christ!

The only way you can fail is if you stop pressing—or if you never even try to begin with. Too many people—even God-fearing Christians—are taking their wild dreams to the grave with them because of a failure mentality. The late American fiction writer Richard Yates once said, "If you don't try at anything, you can't fail...it takes backbone to lead the life you want."[1]

Put in Bible terms, thoughts of failure may try to haunt you, but you can set your face like flint—one of the hardest rocks known to man—believing the God who put the wild dreams in your heart will help you bring them to pass. Isaiah 50:7 reminds us, "For the Lord GOD will help me; therefore, I shall not be disgraced; therefore, I have set my face like a flint, and I know that I shall not be ashamed." God says, "Those who wait for Me shall not be ashamed."

SO WHAT IF YOU FAIL ANYWAY?

Hands down, Michael Jordan is the greatest, most successful, most celebrated basketball player of all time. He scored 32,292 points. He earned six NBA championships. He received five NBA MVP titles and appeared in fourteen All-Star Games.[2] The basketball-loving world still speaks of his jaw-dropping heroics.

But did you know Jordan failed to make the cut of his high school varsity basketball team?[3] What if he let that flop foretell his future? Sports fans everywhere are glad he didn't. He would have robbed the world of one of the greatest-ever athletic talents.

"Whenever I was working out and got tired and figured I ought to stop, I'd close my eyes and see that list in the locker room without my name on it," Jordan said. "That usually got me going again."[4]

Jordan emerged as the star of the junior varsity team, often scoring forty points a game. *Newsweek* reports he averaged a triple-double by his senior year.[5] Despite this success, he kept taking consistent action. Jordan worked hard, played hard, and pulled his team out of many hard situations. All told, he recorded twenty-five game-winning shots, including eight dramatic buzzer-beaters.[6]

Of course he also recorded plenty of lesser-discussed failures. In a Nike commercial Jordan could be heard saying, "I've missed more than nine thousand shots in my career. I've lost almost three hundred games. Twenty-six times, I've been trusted to take the game winning shot and missed. I've failed over and over and over again in my life. And that is why I succeed."[7]

Some of the most celebrated names in history have been miserable failures at some point in their lives. Did you know Apple cofounder Steve Jobs was fired from his own company in 1985? Think about it for a minute. He launched Apple at age twenty-one, became a millionaire by age twenty-three, and was fired at age thirty. Apple brought him back in 1996, and he went on to spearhead the iPod, iPhone, and iWatch—all revolutionary ideas that made Apple a dominant player in the consumer electronics world.[8]

Another modern technology genius, Bill Gates, was a Harvard dropout. His first startup business, Traf-O-Data, was a colossal bomb.[9] He didn't let that stop him from dreaming wild. Instead, Gates pioneered a software company called Microsoft and revolutionized the personal-computing industry. Albert Einstein didn't speak fluently until age nine, was expelled from school, and was initially denied entrance into the Zurich Polytechnic School, but he went on to win the Nobel Prize in physics in 1921.[10]

Colonel Harland Sanders of Kentucky Fried Chicken fame was a sixth-grade dropout. He finally found success with his chicken restaurant, but all too soon construction of a highway devastated his business and left him in dire straits at age sixty-six.[11] He had a dream to sell his recipe and franchise his brand but was turned down over a thousand times.[12] Today over twenty thousand restaurants bear his likeness.[13]

When you read these types of stories, you have to ask yourself, *So what* if I fail? C. S. Lewis, a Christian apologist and British novelist, once said, "Failures are finger posts on the road to achievement."[14] Irish playwright and critic George Bernard Shaw said, "A life spent making mistakes is not only more honorable but more useful than a life spent in doing nothing."[15] And Napoleon Hill said, "More than five hundred of the most successful men this country has ever known... [said] their greatest success came just one step beyond the point at which defeat had overtaken them. Failure is a trickster with a keen sense of irony and cunning. It takes great delight in tripping one when success is almost within reach."[16]

The key to failing well is failing forward. We typically learn more from our failures than from our successes—and when we do fail, our failures pave the way for future success. Music legend Johnny Cash put it this way: "You build on failure. You use it as a stepping-stone. Close the door on the past. You don't try to forget the mistakes, but you don't dwell on it. You don't let it have any of your energy, or any of your time, or any of your space."[17] And author and motivational speaker Zig Ziglar once said, "It's not how far you fall, but how high you bounce that counts."[18]

GOD WILL NOT FAIL YOU

Set out toward your wild dreams with the mind-set that you cannot fail because you will not quit. Even if you fail to hit a milestone— or even if your dream business goes bankrupt—determine now that it's not a failure. It's feedback.

Beyond everything, knowing with all your heart that God is on your side and He will never leave you nor forsake you—or fail you—will give you the courage to press on when it feels as if all is lost. Consider these verses, and let faith arise that the God who put His desires for your life in your heart will surely stand with you, even if you stumble.

> Deuteronomy 20:4—"For the LORD your God is He that goes with you, to fight for you against your enemies, to save you."

> Joshua 10:8—"The LORD said to Joshua, 'Do not be afraid of them, for I have given them into your hand. Not a single man can stand before you.'"

> Proverbs 24:16—"For a just man falls seven times and rises up again, but the wicked will fall into mischief."

Jeremiah 29:11—"For I know the plans that I have for you, says the LORD, plans for peace and not for evil, to give you a future and a hope."

John 16:33—"I have told you these things so that in Me you may have peace. In the world you will have tribulation. But be of good cheer. I have overcome the world."

Romans 8:31–32—"What then shall we say to these things? If God is for us, who can be against us? He who did not spare His own Son, but delivered Him up for us all, how shall He not with Him also freely give us all things?"

Philippians 2:13—"For God is the One working in you, both to will and to do His good pleasure."

Philippians 4:13—"I can do all things because of Christ who strengthens me."

Let Hebrews 13:5 drive home the point that God is faithful and will not fail you: "I will not in any way fail you nor give you up nor leave you without support. [I will] not, [I will] not, [I will] not in any degree leave you helpless nor forsake nor let [you] down (relax My hold on you)! [Assuredly not!]" (AMPC).

God will not fail you, but if you should stumble, let the words of Zig Ziglar echo in your heart: "Remember that failure is an event, not a person."[19] You may fail, but you are not a failure in Christ. And again, you cannot fail if you do not quit.

DREAM WILD EXERCISE: IMAGINE TOTAL VICTORY

The new agers have perverted the concept of imagination with visualization concepts based on what *people* want rather than what God wants. There's nothing wrong with using your holy imagination to see yourself walking in God's will for your life. Imagine yourself reaching your goals—seeing your wild dreams come true. By imagining your success in Christ, you are creatively renewing your mind. You are rooting out vain imaginations of failure. See yourself succeeding at what God has told you to do, and refuse to imagine any other result.

WHAT IF YOU HAD NO FEARS?

The Holy Spirit is saying, "You are going to be OK.
I know sometimes you get anxious about what the
future holds. But you don't have to worry because
Father holds your future in His hands, and His
thoughts toward you are good. Rest assured that He
plans to prosper you and not harm you. He plans to
give you a hope and a future in His kingdom that
is far above anything you can even dream. So don't
worry about tomorrow. Our grace is sufficient."

THINK ABOUT THE question in the chapter title for a moment. What would you do if you had no fears? What would you do if that subtle nagging thought of losing everything was suddenly gone? What if you didn't fear the disapproval of your family and friends? What if you didn't fear transitioning out of the known into the unknown? What if you were fearless?

WHAT IF . . . ?

Although we talked previously about fear as a fierce enemy, part of setting your mind free to dream wild is imagining what you would actually do if fear were out of the equation. Again, fear is often so subtle it's difficult to discern. Fear is deceptive. Sometimes you can't see it until you see it, and even when you do see it, you have a nagging feeling you'll never overcome it. Consider these common fears and what your life would be like if you eradicated these anxieties from your life.

What if you didn't fear financial loss?

Financial loss is one of the most intimidating dream killers. In the face of this fear keep telling yourself, "If God gave me the dream, He will provide the resources to move it forward." God owns everything. You are only a steward. If you step out in faith toward your wild dream and experience loss, the One who put the desire in your heart will make it up to you—and sometimes what looks like loss is a lesson learned or a seed sown toward a harvest you can't yet see.

Fear of financial loss drives us to serve mammon instead of serving the God of our dreams. Decide right now you will not allow the false god named mammon to control you, and you'll see that faith to pursue your dreams will begin to arise. Meditate on Psalm 34:4: "I sought the LORD, and He answered me, and delivered me from all my fears."

What if you didn't fear saying no?

If you are afraid to say no, ask the Holy Spirit why that word frightens your heart. You may have a people-pleasing mind-set you need to overcome. You may be scared of the sting of rejection. Or you may be so mercy oriented that you just can't bear not to lend a hand when you see a need that hasn't been met.

You don't have to be Superman or Wonder Woman. Even Jesus withdrew to the wilderness and prayed sometimes (Luke 5:15–16). I've heard it said that rest is part of the anointing—and rest is available in Christ. You just have to choose to enter into it. Refuse to fear setting boundaries, and you'll move more quickly toward your wild dreams. Meditate on Psalm 56:3–4: "In the day when I am afraid, I will trust in You. In God whose word I praise, in God I have trusted; I will not fear. What can mere flesh do to me?"

What if you didn't fear being the real you?

Rejection works subtly to destroy your self-esteem and your purpose. Rejection causes you to feel sorry for yourself. Rejection spurs you to reject other people before they have an opportunity to reject you. Rejection wants you to base your worth on what you do instead of who you are in Christ.

The spirit of rejection can twist your perception of circumstances so it looks and feels as if you are being rejected even when you aren't. In the natural it's called a misunderstanding. Determine in your heart that you will not be afraid to be the real you—and to be all you can be—and you'll keep progressing toward your dream. Meditate on Psalm 27:1: "The LORD is my light and my salvation; whom will I fear? The LORD is the strength of my life; of whom will I be afraid?"

What if you didn't fear the unknown?

Some people are exhilarated by the unknown. Christopher Columbus, the Spaniard who set sail to discover new lands, was among them. But most of us let fear creep in when we can't see the end from the beginning. We don't have to fear the unknown because we know the One who knows everything. You can purpose in your soul to resist all notions of fearing the unknown and keep your mind on Jesus, who promises to keep you in perfect peace (Isa. 26:3). Meditate on Joshua 1:9: "Have not I commanded you? Be strong and courageous. Do not be afraid or dismayed, for the LORD your God is with you wherever you go."

What if you didn't fear success?

Sounds kind of silly, doesn't it? Who doesn't want to succeed? But you may have a secret fear of success. One of the hidden drivers of this fear is concern about losing relationships. You've heard the saying, "It's lonely at the top." Another hidden fear driving this thought process is anxiety about the persecution or judgment that often comes with success. Ultimately it's about what people will think or do. Fear of man brings a snare to our wild dreams. Meditate on Proverbs 29:25: "The fear of man brings a snare, but whoever puts his trust in the LORD will be safe."

A FEARLESS MIND-SET

Now that we've addressed some of the most common fears that come against your wild dreams, let's take some time to explore how a fearless mind-set could change every area of our lives. Sincerely think about how fearlessness would impact you and those around you using the classic "who, what, when, where, why, and how" line of questioning journalists use in their reporting.

Who would you really be if you were fearless?

What if you had no fear of being misunderstood, rejected, or judged? How would that change your personality? How would it change the way you interact with people? What new relationships might you form if you didn't worry about how you would be perceived? What if the world could see the real you?

You were created in Christ's image—and He considers you a masterpiece (Eph. 2:10). He loves you just the way you are, and He also likes you a whole lot. Receive the love of God, love yourself, love other people, and be the real you—then your dreams will be closer than you think. Meditate on Romans 8:38–39: "For I am persuaded that neither death nor life, neither angels nor principalities nor powers, neither things present nor things to come, neither height nor depth, nor any other created thing, shall be able to separate us from the love of God, which is in Christ Jesus our Lord."

What would you do if you were fearless?

This question is in line with the title of this chapter. What would you do if you had no fear? Really think about it. Let me phrase the question another way to jolt your thinking: If you could do anything in the world you wanted, and you didn't have to consider how anyone would think or feel about it or potential negative consequences of any kind, what would you do? God's wild dream for your life could be found in your honest answer. Meditate on John 14:27: "Peace I leave with you. My peace I give to you. Not as the world gives do I give to you. Let not your heart be troubled, neither let it be afraid."

When would you act if you were fearless?

If you had no fear, when would you act on your wild dreams? I submit that if you were completely fearless, you would take consistent action toward your wild dreams right now. Meditate on Isaiah 12:2: "Certainly God is my salvation; I will trust and not be afraid; for the LORD GOD is my strength and my song; He also has become my salvation."

Where would you work if you were fearless?

We're talking about your dream job. If you didn't fear failure or financial issues, what kind of job would you have? While we need to consider gifts and talents, we must also consider the passion of our hearts. Maybe you're working in an office, but you dream of saving lives. Maybe you can't go to medical school and become a doctor at this stage in your life, but you could be an EMT or at least volunteer at the fire department.

Who knows what door that would open. Meditate on Isaiah 41:10: "Do not fear, for I am with you; do not be dismayed, for I am your God. I will strengthen you, I will help you, yes, I will uphold you with My righteous right hand."

Why would you delay if you were fearless?

The Bible says, "Now faith is" (Heb. 11:1). Faith is now. If you have no fear and you have a green light from God, why would you delay? If you sense any delay in your heart other than God's caution signs, you are allowing fear to put your promises on pause. If you were fearless, you would run to the battle line as David did and take out the Goliath standing between you and your victory. Meditate on Romans 8:15: "For you have not received the spirit of slavery again to fear. But you have received the Spirit of adoption, by whom we cry, 'Abba, Father.'"

How would you proceed if you were fearless?

If no trace of fear remained in your soul, how would you proceed toward your wild dream? What step would you take right now? What plans would you put in place? Where would you invest your time and other resources? What would you do next? Meditate on Psalm 23:1–4: "The LORD is my shepherd; I shall not want. He makes me lie down in green pastures; He leads me beside still waters. He restores my soul; He leads me in paths of righteousness for His name's sake. Even though I walk through the valley of the shadow of death, I will fear no evil; for You are with me; Your rod and Your staff, they comfort me."

Based on the answers to the previous questions, you have a field report for fearless action. Your answers paint a picture of the real you—the fearless you God made you to be. Now put on Christ (Rom. 13:14) and be that person. Henry Ford once said, "One of the greatest discoveries a man makes, one of his great surprises, is to find he can do what he was afraid he couldn't do."[1]

DREAM WILD EXERCISE:
MAKE A FEARLESS LIST

You've probably heard of a bucket list—things you want to do one day before you die. I challenge you today to make a fearless list—things you would do if you were absolutely delivered of fear. This exercise will force you to consider the fears that are holding you back from your wild dreams in every area of your life.

Maybe you would share the secrets of your heart with your best friend if you weren't afraid of being judged. Maybe you would go after that dream job if you didn't fear financial consequences. Maybe you would share your struggles if you didn't fear being rejected. Maybe you would pursue education in a new field if you didn't fear the unknown. What would you do if you were fearless? Start making that list, and face your fears.

WRITE THE VISION AND MAKE IT PLAIN

The Holy Spirit is saying, "That voice you hear telling you that you can't do what I've told you to do is not Me. Why would I call you into this new thing and fail to supply the grace, resources, and connections you need to complete your assignment? Shut out the enemy's voice, and meditate on what I've told you. As you do, you will receive more revelation on how to move forward and the courage to do it. Keep the vision before you no matter what you encounter, and you will overcome and overtake all."

THE LORD SPOKE to the prophet Habakkuk and said, "Write the vision, and make it plain on tablets, that he who reads it may run" (Hab. 2:2). It's one thing to have a dream; it's another thing to write out the vision, make it plain, and start running toward it. Writing out the vision and keeping it before you— reading and visualizing it often—will keep you focused, motivated, and moving toward your wild dreams.

It's important to understand how your dreams and vision work together. A dream is the purpose or goal you're striving for. A vision is seeing how you are going to get from where you are to where God wants you to go.

Although we see in part and know in part (1 Cor. 13:9), we can set our hearts to see everything God wants to show us, knowing part of the Holy Spirit's ministry is to show us things to come. We can also meditate on the parts we do see, believing that God will give us greater understanding and show us more as we need to know it. In His wisdom God knows that if He gave us supernatural vision into the big picture—which would include every skirmish, battle, and war against our dreams—we'd faint before we got started.

God's ways are higher than our ways (Isa. 55:8–9). He usually shows us only the outcome to motivate us to start the journey. As we keep His vision before us, He helps us navigate down the road to destiny when devils emerge from behind the doorknobs he's called us to turn. When we trust Him to bring the vision to pass at the appointed time, we will walk through the holy thresholds to make divine connections.

WHAT THE BIBLE SAYS ABOUT VISION

God is a God of vision, so it's only natural—or should we say supernatural—that His Word shares many verses on the importance of vision. Before we move on to the practical steps for writing out a vision, let's be clear on Scripture:

> "Where there is no vision, the people perish" (Prov. 29:18). The Message translation says, "If people can't see what God is doing, they stumble all over themselves; but when they attend to what He reveals, they are most blessed." The enemy who comes to steal, kill, and destroy your dreams is on the prowl. You must keep the vision before your eyes and in your heart so you don't stumble over enemy thoughts that will undoubtedly plague your mind.

> "For the vision is yet for an appointed time; but it speaks of the end, and does not lie. If it delays, wait for it; it will surely come, it will not delay" (Hab. 2:3). We have to keep the vision ever before us because it's likely we'll lose heart and faint while waiting for it if we don't constantly

remind ourselves of what God said. Delays are almost always a reality. Setbacks can stand in our way and discourage our hearts. But if we keep our eyes on the finish line and know that God is not a man that He should lie or the son of man that He should repent (Num. 23:19), we can encourage ourselves in the Lord.

"The word that came to Jeremiah from the Lord, saying: Thus says the Lord God of Israel: Write all the words that I have spoken to you in a book" (Jer. 30:1–2). In the midst of very dire circumstances, when it seemed as if all were lost, God spoke these words to Jeremiah. In fact, Israel was under judgment when God prophesied through him. Writing the vision down and reviewing it often will charge your faith.

"They said, 'Get up! Let us go up against them, for we have seen the land. It is very good. You are silent, but do not hesitate to go to take the land'" (Judg. 18:9). When you've written down the vision—and once you've visualized with your holy imagination the dream God gave you coming true—you will not hesitate to battle for your promised land. You will not hesitate to go and take the land. Once you truly see it, you'll be willing to go after it.

Helen Keller once said, "The only thing worse than being blind is having sight and no vision."[1] You can have the wildest of wild dreams, but if you don't keep that vision in front of you day and night, your success could be delayed or even derailed. The late Myles Munroe put it this way: "I think that the greatest gift God ever gave man is not the gift of sight but the gift of vision. Sight is a function of the eyes, but vision is a function of the heart."[2] Never let what you see with your eyes defy the desires—the vision—God has put in your heart. And Charles Swindoll summed it up like this: "When you have vision it affects your attitude. Your attitude is optimistic rather than pessimistic."[3]

KEEP GOD'S VISION BEFORE YOU

So how do you make the vision plain? There are time-tested strategies for keeping the vision clear. Here are eight ways to keep the vision alive in your mind, will, emotions, and spirit:

1. Write it out.

We talked about this earlier, but write out your vision, and then post it everywhere you can. Post your vision on your mirror so it confronts you while you are brushing your teeth. Post it on your refrigerator so it reminds you when you go grab a cold drink. Post it on your car dashboard so you glimpse it when you turn the key in the ignition. James Allen, an eighteenth-century British philosophical writer known for his inspirational books, once said, "Dream lofty dreams, and as you dream, so shall you become. Your Vision is the promise of what you shall one day be; your Ideal is the prophecy of what you shall at last unveil."[4]

2. Create a vision board.

Vision boards are fun—and helpful in making the vision plain and keeping it before you. My first vision board had pictures cut out from a magazine, displaying the vision for my life. I had a photo of a stack of books, representing my vision to become a prolific writer for Jesus. I had a photo of a warrior in armor, representing my vision to war in the spirit with expertise. I had a photo of a globe with a plane flying around it, representing my vision to travel internationally with the gospel.

Gather some magazines, or print images off the internet that represent God's wild dream for your life. Paste them to a poster board, and put it somewhere you can see it every day. Let it remind you of what God has put in your heart. The late essayist and poet Henry David Thoreau once wrote, "If one advances confidently in the direction of his dreams, and endeavors to live the life which he has imagined, he will meet with a success unexpected in common hours."[5]

3. Create electronic reminders.

I have set my computer screen saver to float my vision and goals across the screen so when I come back from a break, my vision is speaking to me. You can also set a reminder on your smartphone that prompts you to read your vision again. These reminders can help create a sense of urgency that inspires consistent action. Leonardo da Vinci, an Italian Renaissance polymath, once said, "I have been impressed with the urgency of doing. Knowing is not enough; we must apply. Being willing is not enough; we must do."[6]

4. Think about your vision.

Spend time thinking about your vision—about the dream God has put on your heart. Roll over in your mind what the Lord said. Consider the big picture as you work through the minor details. Now think bigger. As the dream wild prophecy said, "Take the limits off. Take the lid off." Think about the possibilities of the vision rather than the impossibilities of the vision. Best-selling author Davis J. Schwartz puts it this way: "Think progress, believe in progress, push for progress. Think improvement in everything you do."[7]

5. Talk about your vision.

Although you want to be careful not to cast your pearls before swine, you should constantly talk about and cast your vision with people on your team. Sometimes initial naysayers become your biggest cheerleaders once they catch the vision and see your dogged determination. Andy Stanley, son of megachurch pastor Charles Stanley, put it this way: "Casting a convincing vision once is not enough to make it stick. Twice isn't enough either. Vision needs to be repeated regularly."[8]

6. Journal about your vision.

Keep a journal about what God is showing you as the vision—the wild dream—unfolds. Write about your setbacks and the lessons you've learned. Write about your successes along the way with gratitude. As the late British poet William Wordsworth once said, "Fill your paper with the breathings of your heart."[9]

7. Become one with His vision.

Make decisions based on how they will impact the vision; eat, sleep, and breathe the vision. Demonstrate by your actions your commitment to the vision. Jesus was so committed to the vision of seeing the world saved that He died on a cross. You'll never have to go that far, but you may have to die to self, to some degree, to see your dreams come true. The great evangelist Billy Graham would tell you: "Make sure of your commitment to Jesus Christ, and seek to follow Him every day. Don't be swayed by the false values and goals of this world, but put Christ and His will first in everything you do."[10]

8. Pray about your vision.

This should go without saying, as prayer is the foundation of every successful life. Pray about your vision. Pray about it fervently, unceasingly. Pray about it day and night. The Lord will reveal the next step before it's time to take it when you stay close to Him. Nineteenth-century writer, teacher, and pastor Andrew Murray once said, "Prayer is not monologue, but dialogue. God's voice in response to mine is its most essential part."[11]

John C. Maxwell reminds us of an important lesson when it comes to vision: "Failed plans should not be interpreted as a failed vision. Visions don't change, they are only refined. Plans rarely stay the same, and are scrapped or adjusted as needed. Be stubborn about the vision, but flexible with your plan."[12]

DREAM WILD EXERCISE:
CONFESS THE SCRIPTURES

Once God has given you a vision, take some time to find scriptures in the Word of God you can stand on as you run toward it. Find stories of heroes in the Bible who stepped out in faith. Find proverbs that offer wisdom in the journey. Find promises that edify you as you battle the world, the flesh, and the devil to see your wild dreams come true—then confess them daily.

CREATE A SPIRIT-LED PLAN

The Holy Spirit is saying, "Stay in close fellowship
with Me, and I will show you the next steps in My
plan for you. It will be clear. Don't worry. You
won't miss your destiny in the midst of the chaos
that sometimes surrounds you. The promises Father
has made to you will come to pass if you act in faith.
Press in and refuse to shrink back even in the face
of opposition from man and beast. No one can steal
your destiny. No one can stop My will in your life
but you. Stick close to Me. I will lead you there."

YOU'VE HEARD THE world's clichés about planning: "The best-laid plans have gone to waste" or "Everything that can go wrong will go wrong" or "The devil is in the details." The truth is God-laid plans will never go to waste—they will always prosper.

When God speaks a dream to your heart, you can be sure He has a winning plan. Isaiah 55:10–11 assures us: "For as the rain comes down, and the snow from heaven, and do not return there but water the earth and make it bring forth and bud that it may give seed to the sower and bread to the eater, so shall My word be that goes forth from My mouth; it shall not return to Me void, but it shall accomplish that which I please, and it shall prosper in the thing for which I sent it."

God's plans are perfect (Ps. 18:30). The Holy Spirit leads and guides us into all truth and shows us things to come so we stay on God's path, avoiding wrong turns. (See John 16:13.) And yes, I suppose the devil is in the details to some extent, but we have authority over the enemy, in Jesus's name.

Creating a Spirit-led plan to see your wild dreams come true starts with understanding what the Bible says about plans. Armed with a knowledge of Scripture, you can develop a faith-inspiring divine blueprint so detailed it leaves no room for the devil's darts to penetrate. World-famous Spanish painter Pablo Picasso once said, "Our goals can only be reached through a vehicle of a plan, in which we must fervently believe, and upon which we must vigorously act. There is no other route to success."[1]

GOD'S PERFECTED PLANS FOR YOUR WILD DREAMS

We know God's will is good, perfect, and acceptable (Rom. 12:2)—that makes His plans good, perfect, and acceptable. The psalmist understood this as he wrote, "Your eyes saw me unformed, yet in Your book all my days were written, before any of them came into being" (Ps. 139:16). Jesus is not only the Alpha and the Omega; He is the beginning and the end—and He sees your beginning, your end, and all your days in between.

In the midst of judgment God prophesied to Israel words we should keep in mind as we journey toward our wild dreams. I've cited these earlier in the book, but they are worth repeating. Indeed, I believe these are key scriptures to meditate on as you pursue God's dreams for your life: "For I know the plans that I have for you, says the LORD, plans for peace and not for evil, to give you a future and a hope" (Jer. 29:11). The truth is, "'Eye has not seen, nor ear heard, nor has it entered into the heart of man the things which God has prepared for those who love Him.' But God has revealed them to us by His Spirit" (1 Cor. 2:9–10).

When God reveals the dream of His heart for your life, you can know with confidence He will make a way for you to walk in the fullness of that dream. The challenge, at times, is discovering His plan because His thoughts are higher than our thoughts and His ways are higher than our ways (Isa. 55:8–9). But if we press into His wisdom, we will find His plan.

Proverbs 21:5 reminds us, "Good planning and hard work lead to prosperity, but hasty shortcuts lead to poverty" (NLT). Proverbs 16:3 gives us a key to success: "Commit your actions to the LORD, and your plans will succeed" (NLT). And Proverbs 19:21 offers this wisdom: "There are many plans in a man's heart, nevertheless the counsel of the LORD will stand."

If you rush ahead without planning, you are asking for demonic interference. Benjamin Franklin rightly said, "By failing to prepare, you are preparing to fail."[2] Abraham Lincoln gave us a prophetic picture of the power of planning, "Give me six hours to chop down a tree, and I will spend the first four sharpening the ax."[3] And baseball legend Yogi Berra aptly stated, "If you don't know where you're going, you'll end up someplace else."[4]

NINE WAYS TO PLAN A PATH TO WILD DREAM FULFILLMENT

If you haven't noticed already, there is a war for your God-given dreams. Planning is vital to thwarting the enemy's assignment—and the resistance from your own carnal nature—as you walk on God's path. Luke 14:28–32 offers some scriptural insight we would do well to heed:

> For who among you, intending to build a tower, does not sit down first and count the cost to see whether he has resources to complete it? Otherwise, perhaps, after he has laid the foundation and is not able to complete it, all who see it will begin to mock him, saying, "This man began to build and was not able to complete it." Or what king, going to wage war against another king, does not sit down first and take counsel whether he is able with ten thousand to meet him who comes against him with twenty thousand? Otherwise, while the other is yet at a distance, he sends a delegation and requests conditions of peace.

Planning is akin to a prophetic warfare act. General George S. Patton put it this way: "A good plan violently executed now is better than a perfect plan executed next week."[5] Dwight D. Eisenhower, a five-star general during World War II who later became president of the United States, had a similar thought: "In preparing for battle, I have always found that plans are useless but planning is indispensable."[6]

1. Strategize in prayer.

The Holy Spirit is omniscient. He always has the best strategy, which is why it is crucial that you strategize in prayer. Brainstorm with the Holy Spirit. Ask Him for wisdom, guidance, counsel— ask Him for the blueprint. Ask Him to give you a heads-up about the enemy's tactics to counter your dreams so you can break the power of any and all opposition. Ask Him to order your steps. Ask Him to help you set your priorities. Ask Him to show you things to come. The Holy Spirit is our helper.

After you've prayed all this and more, pray in the Spirit. Paul shared a marvelous revelation in 1 Corinthians 14:2: "For he who speaks in an unknown tongue does not speak to men, but to God. For no one understands him, although in the spirit, he speaks mysteries." I pray in the Spirit as much as I possibly can. I wake up most mornings and pray at least thirty minutes in the Spirit before doing anything else. I pray in the Spirit while I am in my car. I even broke out in tongues on the treadmill at the gym accidentally—because it's automatic. I'm not telling you this to create a law, but to encourage you to allow praying in the Spirit to become so natural that your immediate response in times of need is to lift up Spirit-led prayers.

Paul offers a revelation that can change your entire life in Romans 8:26: "Likewise, the Spirit helps us in our weaknesses, for we do not know what to pray for as we ought, but the Spirit Himself intercedes for us with groanings too deep for words." We may think we know how to pray, and sometimes we do, but many times we don't have a clue what prayer answer we really need. If you are not getting prayer answers, consider what James 4:3 says about asking "amiss." The Greek word for "amiss" in this scripture can be translated "improperly" or "wrongly."[7] If you are praying wrongly, you won't get the right answers—or perhaps any answer.

Paul continues the revelation in Romans 8:27: "He who searches the hearts knows what the mind of the Spirit is, because He intercedes for the saints according to the will of God." The Holy Spirit has the mind of God. He always knows the perfect will of the Father and always gets His prayers answered. Let Him help you pray, and you will surely tap into the 1 John 5:14–15 promise: "This is the confidence that we have in Him, that if we ask anything according to His will, He hears us. So if we know that He hears whatever we ask, we know that we have whatever we asked of Him."

2. Break down your master plan into action steps.

Once you have your plan, you need to break down the big picture into what I call puzzle pieces. While it's important to see the big picture, it's equally important to understand every piece you'll need to gather and assemble to create the scenery about which you are dreaming.

While you need wisdom from God, there is also natural reasoning on what you should do first, next, and after that. I've learned to start with the end in mind. Of course I also think from beginning to end about each progressive step it will take to hit the goal. Ultimately I've found that looking at the big picture from both directions helps me avoid skipping steps along the way.

I break down projects into phases. There's a preparation phase and an execution phase. It's good to prepare everything you can but not to the point of perfectionism or paralyzation. In other words, preparation is strategic, but too much preparation can pave the way for the devil to get into the details and delay your wild dreams. The important thing is to keep moving forward—to drive consistent action—toward the master plan.

3. Consider who else may need to be involved.

Is God calling others to work alongside you? Whose favor do you need to open doors for you? What expertise do you need to gain from people who are more knowledgeable than you? Do you need intercessors backing you up? Do you need to hire people? Consider these questions, and then pray that God will help you make the right connections.

4. Consider what financial resources are required.

The enemy will use money—or lack thereof—to overwhelm you. You may have to resist those feelings as you consider the financial resources that may be required to bring your dream into reality. Count the costs. If you are investing in yourself, a business, or a church, how much do you need to invest to drive the dream forward? You can't pray specific prayers for provision without first counting the costs.

5. Set clear deadlines.

Goals without deadlines are just wishes. Always set a clear deadline for each action step or goal. If you miss the mark, extend the goal but keep the deadline before you. Deadlines generate a sense of urgency.

6. Find an accountability partner.

Accountability partners are helpful in executing your plan. Find someone, if you can, who will challenge you without nagging you, someone you can check in with each week to share your progress toward your goals. Just knowing you are going to have that weekly meeting will help you stay on track.

7. Receive wise counsel.

Proverbs 15:22 says, "Without counsel, purposes are disappointed, but in the multitude of counselors they are established." The Holy Spirit is your Counselor, but He can and does speak through other people. Take all the counsel you can get, and then pray about it before moving into it.

8. Celebrate milestones toward your dreams.

When you accomplish a significant task—when you turn a critical corner or reach a goal—celebrate. Give yourself a pat on the back. Take a day off to rest. Go out to dinner. Do something fun. Reward yourself for your diligence.

9. Review feedback along the way.

Feedback is vital. It tells us when we are on the right path or when we need to ramp up spiritual warfare against the opposition. If what you are doing is not working, one of two things is likely happening: you are doing the wrong things, or you are being massively opposed. Discern the issue, and either change your activities or wage war against the spiritual enemy working to stop your forward movement.

DREAM WILD EXERCISE:
PRAY IN THE SPIRIT

Romans 8:26 says, "Likewise, the Spirit helps us in our weaknesses, for we do not know what to pray for as we ought, but the

Spirit Himself intercedes for us with groanings too deep for words." Before you set out to create your Spirit-inspired plan, take some time to pray in the Spirit and pray in your earthly language as well. If you want to be led by the Spirit, you need to calm your soul, pray, and then listen. Many times the Lord will inspire our hearts with witty, inventive ideas when we pray, pray, and pray some more. Praying in the Spirit, as Paul said, unlocks mysteries.

DAY 28

WRITE OUT ACTIONABLE GOALS

The Holy Spirit is saying, "Your God-given dreams can come true, but you have to pursue the God who gave you the dreams. You also have to take Spirit-led action in faith toward your godly goals. Yes, you'll meet with spiritual warfare and natural stumbling blocks and be tempted to give up. But don't give up! Don't give in. If you seek first the kingdom of God and My will for your life, you will see your dreams manifest in Father's timing. Just keep pressing in! I am with you!"

MOSES HAD A goal to deliver the children of Israel from the bondage of the Egyptians. David had a goal to defeat Goliath. Esther had a goal to save her people from Haman's destructive plan. Throughout the pages of the Bible, we find characters with crystal-clear, actionable goals. We find them, as Paul so eloquently wrote, pressing "toward the goal to the prize" (Phil. 3:14).

Every wild dreamer needs to establish short- and long-term goals on her field of dreams. Whether or not you're a football fan, you understand that any team's goal is to win the game. But that overarching goal is made up of many smaller goals, such as getting a first down (advancing the ball at least ten yards down the field within four plays), getting a touchdown, kicking a field goal, and stopping the opposing team from doing all those things.

I'm a list maker. I love lists because they help me stay on track with my goals. Each year I make a list of life goals—even things I'd like to do one day for fun. I make a list of annual goals—which always starts with getting closer to God à la Matthew 6:33. I make a list of monthly, weekly, daily, and even hourly goals. That may sound like overkill to you, but I've realized that goals are a vital ingredient in the recipe for success. A day without actionable goals is like baking a cake without flour. It falls flat.

Writing out actionable goals—goals you can take action on—requires you to see the end from the beginning. In other words, you need to determine what to do first, what to do next, and what not to do at all as you encounter competing goals that will lead to that touchdown and your ultimate victory on the field of dreams.

Whatever your dream is, take some time before you start pressing toward it to consider the short- and long-term goals. Short-term goals are what you need to do today, this week, this month, or this quarter to take you closer to your dream. Long-term goals are what you need to do this year or in the years ahead to see your dream come true. Start by defining your long-term goals and break out all the activities you need to reach the dream goal. Those activities translate into short-term goals.

As I said, actionable goals are goals you can take action on, but let's explore that concept a little further. Actionable goals are the opposite of ambiguous goals. An ambiguous goal lacks clarity. When your goals lack clarity, you can end up with the wrong result. Ambiguous goals are vague and have no deadline. Goals without deadlines are merely wishes. Actionable goals are clear. You are saying, "I plan to accomplish this specific action by this specific date."

SETTING SMART GOALS

When it comes to goal-setting, SMART is a good place to start. This concept emerged in the November 1981 issue of *Management Review*. George T. Doran is credited with coining the mnemonic acronym, which stands for specific, measurable, achievable, results-focused, and time-related.[1] This is truly the foundation for actionable goals. Let's break this down for clarity's sake.

Specific

As you write out your goals, be as specific as possible. Write goals using simple language that leaves no room for interpretation. Clearly define the dream you want to achieve as you understand it currently. If your goal is to serve on the mission field, you might write something like this: "I will step onto the mission field with a reputable organization that has the infrastructure necessary to reach as many people as possible with the gospel of Jesus Christ." If your goal is to build a business, you could write something along these lines: "I will launch a new business based on the innovative idea God gave me about _____."

Measurable

You won't know if you are moving toward your goal—and the realization of your dream—if you don't measure your progress. A goal that cannot be measured is not clear enough because you will not know whether you've hit the mark. Adding a deadline to your goal makes it measurable. To set a deadline is to set a time or date to accomplish the goal. If it's a daily goal, you might have a time of the day by which you need to complete a project. If it's a larger goal, it may be a month and day. Dating your goals leaves no room for wondering if you reached them.

Achievable

Unrealistic goals will discourage you, but goals that don't challenge you to grow in the process of achieving your dreams will delay your progress. Always set the bar higher than the level of your comfort but not so high that you will be intimidated to the point of procrastination. Although all things are possible with God, goals that are too large with deadlines that are too soon are likely to set you up for disappointment—and the enemy will take advantage of the setback.

Results focused

You can easily keep yourself busy with tasks that don't drive you toward your dreams. Every successful dreamer is results oriented. You're not measuring how many items to tick off your to-do list in a day. Busyness is the enemy to fruitfulness. You have to adopt Christ's attitude when He hung on a cross—keep your eyes on the prize. Keep the end in mind. Keep the results you want to achieve at the fore so you don't waste time chasing bright, shiny objects.

Time related

Without a sense of urgency, we're likely to allow the enemy to distract us with good things that are not God things. The same mechanism that helps you measure the realization of your goals also creates this tension. Set a date and time by which you will accomplish each and every goal, and then start pressing forward!

GOAL-SETTING STRATEGIES FOR EVERY DREAMER

As you set out to write down actionable goals, you may feel overwhelmed—particularly if your dream is especially wild. You may not know where to begin. That's OK. There are many strategies to help you set actionable goals.

Use mind mapping.

If you aren't exactly sure how or where to start, a mind map can be strategic. There is mind mapping software on the market, but you can just as easily use a whiteboard, poster board, or notebook to mind-map your dream. This is an especially helpful tool to help you visualize the big picture. Here's how it works: Start with the goal in the middle of the page, and circle it. From there draw branches on the circle that represent the long-term goals associated with the project. Those branches then have subbranches representing specific tasks necessary to accomplish a project that leads you toward your goal. There are entire articles and books written about mind mapping. If this concept sounds interesting to you, it's easy to research it further.

Do a brain dump on paper.

If a mind map sounds too complex for you, you could just dump everything down on paper. Write your dream at the top, and then brainstorm everything that comes to mind—every project, activity, or person you need to help you reach the goal.

Prioritize your goals.

Your long-term and short-term goals could have your head spinning. Now is the time to set priorities. Prioritize your goals in a logical order. Do *this* first, *this* next, *this* third, and so on. Think logically about the sequence of events necessary to accomplish your goal, and then organize them in that order.

Use Google Calendar.

You can use any calendar, but the benefit of an online calendar is you can access it anywhere and update it on the fly. Google Calendar lets you set reminders and deadlines and can help you stay organized and focused on reaching your goals.

Create daily and weekly to-do lists.

Your days and weeks will get away from you if you don't take the time to plan out what you need to accomplish each day and each week. You can use a Daytimer, notebook, or notepad to create these lists.

You'll find an endless list of mobile and web-based apps available to help you set and track goals. Some of these can be helpful, especially if you need to keep a group on track to press forward. However, some of them can be distracting, especially if you are an experienced goal setter. Only you know the best approach to keeping your eyes on the prize and keeping your dreams on track. But no matter your style, goal setting is vital. Zig Ziglar once said, "A goal properly set is halfway reached."[2]

DREAM WILD EXERCISE:
SET A SMART GOAL NOW

Your wild dream will include many goals along the way. Set one goal right now using the SMART method. Then set a few more. Once you get the hang of it, you'll have a series of goals that set the stage for your wild dreams to come true.

TAKE CONSISTENT ACTION

The Holy Spirit is saying, "Your God-given dreams can come true, but you have to pursue the God who gave you the dreams. You also have to take Spirit-led action in faith toward your godly goals. Yes, you'll meet with spiritual warfare and natural stumbling blocks and be tempted to give up. But don't give up! Don't give in. If you seek first the kingdom of God and My will for your life, you will see your dreams manifest in Father's timing. Just keep pressing in! I am with you!"

SEEING YOUR WILD dreams come true demands consistent action. Once you've overcome dream killers such as procrastination and perfectionism, you can begin to cultivate determined consistency in your heart—determined consistency that sees even the wildest dreams through to reality. Put another way, without consistency your dreams will not be established.

Determined, consistent action takes faith—the kind of faith that's a verb as much as it is a noun. In other words, faith that's action oriented. Merriam-Webster's dictionary defines *faith* as "allegiance to duty or a person."[1] Wild dreamers need an allegiance to their God-given imaginations—and the God who gave them the imaginations. It's the kind of faith we read about in James 2:14–18:

What does it profit, my brothers, if a man says he has faith but has no works? Can faith save him? If a brother or sister is naked and lacking daily food, and one of you says to them, "Depart in peace, be warmed and filled," and yet you give them nothing that the body needs, what does it profit? So faith by itself, if it has no works, is dead. But a man may say, "You have faith and I have works." Show me your faith without your works, and I will show you my faith by my works.

True faith drives action—but not just once-in-a-while-when-it's-convenient-and-I-feel-like-it action. True faith drives determined, consistent action. If we look in the Hall of Faith in Hebrews 11, we see this type of faith—the faith that sees dreams come true or dies trying. Consider Noah: "By faith Noah, being divinely warned about things not yet seen, moved with godly fear, prepared an ark to save his family, by which he condemned the world and became an heir of the righteousness that comes by faith" (Heb. 11:7).

Dreaming with God, Noah displayed determined, consistent action despite naysayers who surely surrounded him in an age when it had never rained. I can just imagine Noah taking massive action to build an ark of cypress wood, complete with interior rooms covered inside and out with a pitch and with skeptics surrounding him on all sides. Nevertheless, by faith Noah co-labored with God to see His dream of saving a righteous seed from His wrath come true. Genesis 6:22 tells us Noah did all that God commanded him. Doing all that God commands us requires determined, consistent action.

WHY DETERMINED, CONSISTENT ACTION MATTERS

Success coach Jim Rohn once said, "Success is neither magical nor mysterious. Success is the natural consequence of consistently applying basic fundamentals."[2] Your basic fundamental is faith in the God who put His desires in your heart. When you consistently apply faith with Spirit-led works in any area of your life, you will see success in that area.

Let's look at some simple definitions to drive the point home. According to Merriam-Webster, *consistent* means "marked by harmony, regularity, or steady continuity: free from variation or contradiction; marked by agreement; showing steady conformity to character, profession, belief, or custom."[3] By contrast, *inconsistent* means "lacking consistency; not compatible with another fact or claim; containing incompatible elements; incoherent or illogical in thoughts or actions; not satisfiable by the same set of values for the unknowns."[4]

As you can see, inconsistency can kill your dreams. Consistency is key. Consistent people aren't distracted by the devil or bright, shiny objects that lead them on bunny trails. Consistent people are committed to seeing the dream through to the end. Consistent people have developed strong thought patterns that lead to strong habits. Consistent people are dependable, reliable, and accountable. Consistent people don't offer excuses but stay steady for the long haul, refusing to allow obstacles to sway them. Here are three reasons determined, consistent action is paramount to seeing your wild dreams come true:

1. There is no momentum without consistency. Think about it for a minute. If you are trying to lose weight, you will not succeed without consistent exercise and healthy eating habits. You won't build weight-loss momentum without consistent action. Likewise, you won't keep the weight off long term without a consistent lifestyle change.

2. Consistency creates expertise. There's a learning curve to every new effort. When you begin going down a new path, you have to learn the twists and turns. You may need to acquire new skill sets on the road to seeing your dreams manifest. Just as it takes consistent practice to learn to play a musical instrument or speak a new language, it takes consistent effort to develop the skills you may need to reach your wild dreams.

3. Inconsistency does not please God. When God speaks to you, He expects you to believe Him. Hebrews 11:6 tells us, "And without faith it is

impossible to please God, for he who comes to God must believe that He exists and that He is a rewarder of those who diligently seek Him." And James 1:6–8 says, "But let him ask in faith, without wavering. For he who wavers is like a wave of the sea, driven and tossed with the wind. Let not that man think that he will receive anything from the Lord. A double-minded man is unstable in all his ways."

Finally, when we're inconsistent about doing what God told us to do, we're setting ourselves up to fail because we've deceived ourselves, as James 1:22 explains: "Do not merely listen to the word, and so deceive yourselves. Do what it says" (NIV).

OVERCOMING INCONSISTENCY IN YOUR LIFE

When God puts a wild dream in my heart, I like to get out of the gate and start running as fast as I can—or at least as fast as wisdom dictates. Although attaining your wild dreams is somewhat like a marathon, I start running at breakneck speed when I know that I know that I know it's God who put the dream in my heart. I instantly start pressing toward the goal to win the prize before the enemy has time to organize against me.

Consider Paul's words in 1 Corinthians 9:24–25: "Do you not know that all those who run in a race run, but one receives the prize? So run, that you may obtain it. Everyone who strives for the prize exercises self-control in all things."

Determined consistency requires self-discipline, or self-control, which is a fruit of the Spirit listed in Galatians 5:22–23. The word for self-control in this verse is *egkrateia*, which describes "the virtue of one who masters his desires and passions, especially his sensual appetites."[5] Your fleshly or sensual appetites will derail your wild dreams if you consistently feed them. By contrast, if you consistently display self-control—crucifying the flesh that works against your dreams—you will reach the finish line of your marathon.

Charles Swindoll, a pastor, author, and radio preacher, once wrote:

Consistency.
    It's the jewel worth wearing…
    It's the anchor worth weighing…

It's the thread worth weaving...
It's the battle worth winning.[6]

If you've noticed inconsistency in your life, here are some strategies to overcome this dream killer.

1. Find your motivation deep within your heart. Find your "why" behind the "what." If you can keep in mind why you are doing something—and the why is strong enough—you are more likely to do it with consistency. If your why is not compelling you to take consistent action, you have to question if it's really God's dream for your life. If nothing else, obedience to God should be your motivation.

2. Don't let your emotions lead the way. Your emotions are fickle. You'll feel like pressing toward the mark of the prize one day, and the next day you may wake up feeling discouraged. If I did only what I felt like doing, I would sit on the beach and eat ice cream most days. I spend much of my time doing things I don't feel like doing in order to get where I really want to go.

3. Develop a daily schedule. If there are things you must do consistently to see your wild dreams come true, include them on a daily schedule until those tasks become instinctive. Let your daily schedule serve as a personal trainer of sorts to help you discipline yourself to take consistent action that will move you toward your dreams.

4. Hold yourself accountable. You can find an accountability partner, but ultimately only you can hold yourself accountable to take consistent action toward your wild dreams. While there are some days when you'll need to cut yourself some slack and not set unrealistic goals, you know down deep in your heart the difference between cutting

yourself some slack and slacking. Stay true to your dreams, and your dreams will come true.

An old proverb from an unknown author opines, "Be careful of your thoughts, for your thoughts become your words. Be careful of your words, for your words become your actions. Be careful of your actions, for your actions become your habits. Be careful of your habits, for your habits become your character. Be careful of your character, for your character becomes your destiny."[7]

DREAM WILD EXERCISE: BUILDING STRONG HABITS

A habit is something you do consistently. So how do you build strong habits? First, identify the habit you want to build. Let's say you want to get up earlier in the morning to get a jump start on your goals before the rest of the world wakes up. Every habit you set out to form will depend on consistent actions. Following the example of getting up earlier in the morning, you'll first have to make a firm decision to go to bed earlier and set an alarm to wake you up earlier—and then refuse to hit snooze ten times!

Sometimes we fail to develop strong habits because we don't break them down into smaller steps. If you are currently getting up at 7:00 a.m., for example, and you want to start getting up at 5:00 a.m., you may need to take smaller steps toward your ultimate goal of habitually rising before the crack of dawn. Start with 6:30 a.m., then 6:00 a.m., then 5:30 a.m.

Whatever habit you are working to develop, know that your flesh, other people, and even the devil will try to set you back. If you miss it, get up and try again until the habit becomes so strong internally that external forces won't sway you.

ASK, ASK, ASK

The Holy Spirit is saying, "What would happen if
you simply asked? Is it possible that a miracle would
manifest in your midst if you only asked? What would
happen if you pursued in faith what you think Father
is calling you to do? Is it possible you would exceed
your own wildest dreams? I'm telling you it is possible.
Meditate on this: 'Ask and it will be given to you; seek
and you will find; knock and it will be opened to you.
For everyone who asks receives, and he who seeks
finds, and to him who knocks, it will be opened.' [See
Matthew 7:7–8.] You'll never know if you don't ask."

IN 2014 THE Lord spoke plainly to me about "a year of asking." This was not a corporate word for the body of Christ. This was a personal word of wisdom for me. However, I believe it's a Bible-tested prophetic word for many who are pressing into wild dreams in this hour.

Seriously consider this: Is it possible that you don't have the resources, the relationships, and the open doors that lead to your realized dreams because you aren't asking? James, the apostle of practical faith, suggests failing to ask is tied to failing to receive, at least in some cases. He wrote: "You desire to have and cannot obtain. You fight and war. Yet you do not have, because you do not ask" (James 4:2).

James's sage advice was in the context of prayer, but in my experience—and in biblical reality—God often uses people as a channel to help you get what He wants you to have. Put another way, sometimes you have to ask the people who possess the power to help you for what God has shown you is His will.

When the Holy Spirit told me it was "a year of asking," I took Him at His word. I sought His face, asking what He wanted me to have—what His will for me was in that season—and determined to dream with Him. As I sought His heart, He showed me that specific people hold specific keys to specific doors He wanted me to walk through. He revealed gatekeepers to different platforms He wanted me to step on. And He taught me the principle of humbling myself to ask.

Keep in mind that I did not presume to ask for something God didn't show me was His dream for me in that season. I did not presume to ask people He didn't lead me to just because I thought in my natural mind they could help me see my dreams come true. I let His Spirit lead me—to order my steps to the right place at the right time for the divine connections.

MY ASKING EXPERIMENT

At the same time, I did not allow the voice of fear or rejection—or fear of rejection—to stop me from opening my mouth and asking. I chose to obey the leading of the Lord, understanding that even if someone told me no I was no worse off than I was before I asked— and I refused to get offended or hurt if my request was declined.

On the other hand, if they told me yes, I was advancing toward God's dream for my life. What's more, if God uses someone to help me accomplish His will, there is a blessing in it for everyone. It's a win-win. Who am I to rob someone of his blessings because I'm too big or too scared to ask?

Armed with these revelations, I started asking God—then asking the people He led me to—for everything I was sure He wanted me to pursue. The results were incredible. I'm no math genius, but I would venture to calculate I received 95 percent or more of what I asked for—and I asked for some pretty big things.

One of the most memorable examples happened at Charisma Media. I was in a meeting with the book group discussing book ideas for the following year. Someone in the meeting mentioned having an idea for a devotional and had asked several well-known Christian authors to tackle it, but none felt led of the Lord to say yes. When I heard this, my spirit leaped on the inside of me, but I kept my lips zipped. I prayed and asked the Lord if it was His dream for me in that season to pen this devotional.

Next thing I knew, I was in the elevator with an executive in the book group, and out of my mouth came, "You know that devotional you've been looking for someone to write? I'd like to write it!" I could hardly believe I said it. It was like the Holy Ghost took over my mouth! My personality is very reserved, and I am typically not bold enough to ask people for much, much less for a book opportunity. To my surprise, she said, "That sounds good! Let's do it!"

Of course, we had to go through all the acceptance processes you would with any book acquisition, but I knew in my heart this was part of God's dream for my life. That book is my best-selling book ever, printed in three languages and in audio form. It's called *Mornings With the Holy Spirit: Listening Daily to the Still, Small Voice of God.* It was followed by *Evenings With the Holy Spirit.* God has used this book, and the morning prayer broadcasts associated with it, to touch the lives of hundreds of thousands of people. I would not have had this opportunity—I would not have seen this wild dream come true—if I didn't ask God and ask a person.

MEN SHALL GIVE INTO YOUR BOSOM

We should always ask God for what we need and want even though He already knows what we need before we ask Him (Matt. 6:8). We are to trust in Him as our provider. However, Scripture shows us He uses people as provision agents time and time again.

Consider Jesus's words in Luke 6:38: "Give, and it will be given to you: Good measure, pressed down, shaken together, and running over will men give unto you. For with the measure you use, it will be measured unto you." Notice He said "will men give unto you."

The Lord led the prophet Elijah to ask a woman for a cake of bread during a time of famine. We read the account in 1 Kings 17:7–9: "After some time, the brook dried up because there had been no rain in the land. The word of the LORD came to him, saying, 'Arise, go to Zarephath, which belongs to Sidon, and live there. I have commanded a widow there to provide for you.'"

Elijah didn't hesitate. When he found the widow gathering sticks, he asked her for some water and a morsel of bread. The widow told him she didn't have any bread to offer him, just a handful of meal and a little oil in the jar. Elijah prophesied to her: "Do not fear; go and do as you have said, but make a little cake for me first, and bring it to me, and afterward, make some for your son and you, for thus says the LORD God of Israel: The barrel of meal will not run out, nor will the jar of oil empty, until the day that the LORD sends rain upon the earth" (1 Kings 17:13–14).

This wasn't prophetic manipulation. This was the Spirit of God's mercy working to provide for Elijah, the widow, and her son. The widow obeyed. She said yes. She sought to help provide for Elijah, and the prophecy manifested. Her meal did not run out, and her jar of oil did not run dry.

At times, God will move on people's hearts to give you what He wants you to have. Sometimes, though, people don't discern God's leading until you ask them. Your ask unlocks a revelation that they can and should help.

God can use believers and unbelievers alike to give into your bosom. Again, that doesn't mean you should start trying to break doors down, asking anyone and everyone who you think can help you lend a hand with a pushy spirit. The type of asking we need to subscribe to is Spirit-led asking. The Holy Spirit will show you whom to ask, when to ask, and even how to ask—"The Holy Spirit will teach you at that time what you should say" (Luke 12:12).

Consider these words from an anonymous author:

> A little boy was having difficulty lifting a heavy stone. His father came along just then. Noting the boy's failure, he asked, "Are you using all your strength?"
>
> "Yes, I am," the little boy said impatiently.
>
> "No, you are not," the father answered. "I am right here, just waiting, and you haven't asked me to help you."[1]

DREAM WILD EXERCISE:
PRACTICE THE ART OF ASKING GOD'S WAY

Many people use some subtle form of manipulation or put on the charm when asking people for the help God wants to give them. They may suggest, "If you scratch my back, I'll scratch yours" without saying it. They may try to make you feel sorry for them or guilt you. This is not God's way.

If you are confident God has spoken to you, then you don't have to twist arms, play games, or trade favors. You can ask honestly for the help you need—and graciously give them a way out in the asking. Ask for what you need with a sincere heart, but assure them that saying no will not affect the relationship—and really mean it.

Asking, whether of people or of God, requires humility. And remember Luke 6:38: "Give, and it will be given to you..." You can sow "helping" seeds and expect a "helping" harvest. When the Spirit of God leads you to help someone, do it.

Galatians 6:10 admonishes us: "Therefore, as we have opportunity, let us do good to all people, especially to those who are of the household of faith." And we know that what we make happen for someone else God will make happen for us, according to Ephesians 6:8: "Whatever good thing any man does, he will receive the same from the Lord." Go ahead, start your Spirit-inspired asking!

CONCLUSION

A PRAYER TO ACTIVATE YOUR WILDEST DREAMS

W E STARTED THIS journey reading the dream wild prophetic word. It's only fitting that we review that prophecy as we launch out into prayer. I want to encourage you to meditate on this prophetic word as you pursue your God-given dreams. War with this prophecy according to 1 Timothy 1:18. And pray this prayer as many times as you need to inspire your heart.

Let's review the word again:

> *I am marking you with My glory. I am changing you from the inside out. It's time to embark on a new season of chasing Me. You will be more effective. You will be more efficient. You will do more with less. You can't see it. It's hard for you to believe it, but I am the author of it.*
>
> *Take the limits off. Take the lid off. I am opening new doors for you. It's not just about favor. I'm shifting you from favor to open heavens. You will not strive, but you will not lack. I have gone before you to make a way for you. The divine connections are right around the corner. They are just ahead. You will see them and know them.*
>
> *I am indeed giving you double for your trouble. I will put in your hands as much as you can believe Me for. How much can you believe Me for? Dream again. Dream big dreams. Dream wild dreams. Dream with Me, and I will dream with you.*

Now let's pray:

> *Father, I thank You that You are the God of my dreams—even my wildest dreams. Help me never chase my dreams but chase You and You alone. Help me keep You in the center of my focus so I can stay peaceful when the enemy rises up against the desires You've put in my heart, in Jesus's name.*
>
> *Father, help me yield to the inward working of Your Spirit to change me from glory to glory and move me from faith to faith. Help me see what You see in me so I will have confidence on the hard days to stay the course. Give me an enduring spirit. Give me a steadfast mind. Give me a preserving heart. Help me never let the words "I quit" come out of my mouth. Help me renew my mind so the enemy can't successfully steal, kill, and destroy the dreams You've put in my heart, in Jesus's name.*
>
> *Father, I believe. Help my unbelief. Help me to never doubt You and to exercise my faith. Help me not to be double-minded. Teach me to identify limiting beliefs that are holding me back and develop the disciplines in my life that will forward Your plans for my life. Show me how to overcome the enemies of my wild dreams, from fear to doubt to procrastination. Help me stand strong against the challenges and obstacles to my desires, whether from the spirit or the natural realm, in Jesus's name.*
>
> *Father, teach me to discern the divine connections You have for me as I pursue Your good, perfect, and acceptable will for my life. Surround me with people who will support me, and teach me to be a support to the people around me as they pursue their wild dreams, in Jesus's name.*
>
> *Father, open doors for me that no man can open, and shut any doors that You want shut. Inspire me not to settle for a good thing when there is a God thing in store. Help me not to get impatient in the waiting process, in Jesus's name.*
>
> *Father, keep me from striving, and teach me to walk in Your sufficient grace. Help me not get ahead of You but never lag behind You. Help me dream Your dreams for my life and not my carnal, selfish dreams. Father God, help*

me see my dreams come true so I can glorify Your Son, in Jesus's name.

I say let Your will be done and let Your kingdom come in my life. I activate my faith for an unrelenting pursuit of every dream You have in Your heart for me, in Jesus's name. Amen.

You may also want to pick up a copy of my *Dream Wild* CD, where I declare this prophecy and some additional exhortations against a backdrop of music that will help you memorize the truths in this prophetic word. You can pick up your copy at dreamwild.org.

NOTES

INTRODUCTION
THE WILD PROPHECY THAT RADICALLSY CHANGED MY LIFE

1. *Strong's Exhaustive Concordance of the Bible*, s.v. "charis," Blue Letter Bible, accessed July 6, 2017, https://www.blueletterbible.org/lang/Lexicon /Lexicon.cfm?strongs=G5485&t=KJV.

2. Bible Study Tools, s.v. "Jehovah-Jireh," accessed September 5, 2017, http://www.biblestudytools.com/commentaries/maclaren/genesis/jehovah -jireh.html.

DAY 1
JESUS INVITES YOU TO DREAM WILD

1. *Strong's Exhaustive Concordance of the Bible*, s.v. "an," accessed September 19, 2017, https://www.blueletterbible.org/lang/Lexicon/Lexicon .cfm?strongs=G302&t=KJV.

2. Merriam-Webster.com, s.v. "whatever," accessed September 19, 2017, https://www.merriam-webster.com/dictionary/whatever.

3. *Strong's Exhaustive Concordance of the Bible*, s.v. "tis," accessed September 19, 2017, https://www.blueletterbible.org/lang/Lexicon/Lexicon .cfm?strongs=G5100&t=KJV.

4. Larry Pierce, Outline of Biblical Usage, s.v. "thelō," accessed September 19, 2017, https://www.blueletterbible.org/lang/Lexicon/Lexicon .cfm?strongs=G2309&t=KJV.

5. Merriam-Webster.com, s.v. "all," accessed July 7, 2017, https://www .merriam-webster.com/dictionary/all.

6. Merriam-Webster.com, s.v. "all."

7. *Webster's Revised Unabridged Dictionary*, s.v. "barren," accessed July 7, 2017, http://biblehub.com/topical/b/barren.htm.

8. Leonard C. Schlup and Donald W. Whisenhunt, eds., *It Seems to Me: Selected Letters of Eleanor Roosevelt* (Lexington, KY: The University of Kentucky Press, 2001), 2.

DAY 2
DEVELOPING FAITH TO DREAM WILD

1. Mary McLeod Bethune, "Last Will and Testament," Bethune-Cookman University, accessed November 2, 2017, http://www.cookman .edu/about_BCU/history/lastwill_testament.html.

DAY 3
UNLOCKING YOUR WILD DREAMS WITH HOLY SPIRIT'S HELP

1. *Merriam-Webster*, s.v. "miracle," accessed September 19, 2017, https://www.merriam-webster.com/dictionary/miracle.

2. Matthew Henry, *Matthew Henry's Commentary on the Bible*, Romans Chapter 8, accessed September 19, 2017, https://www.biblegateway.com/resources/matthew-henry/Rom.8.26-Rom.8.28.

3. Johann Wolfgang von Goethe, as quoted on BrainyQuote, accessed September 19, 2017, https://www.brainyquote.com/quotes/quotes/j/johannwolf121252.html.

DAY 4
RELEASING GOD'S WORD OVER YOUR WILD DREAMS

1. *The NAS New Testament Greek Lexicon*, s.v. "sozo," Bible Study Tools, accessed September 19, 2017, http://www.biblestudytools.com/lexicons/greek/nas/sozo.html.

2. T. E. Lawrence, *Seven Pillars of Wisdom* (Ware, UK: Wordsworth Editions Limited, 1997), 7.

DAY 5
DRAWING INSPIRATION FROM WILD DREAMERS

1. John Findling, "World's Fair," *Encyclopædia Britannica*, accessed September 8, 2017, https://www.britannica.com/topic/worlds-fair; "Fairground Rides—A Chronological Development," University of Sheffield, accessed September 19, 2017, https://web.archive.org/web/20110811021142/https://www.nfa.dept.shef.ac.uk/history/rides/history.html.

2. "Coney Island History: The Story of Captain Paul Boyton and Sea Lion Park," David A. Sullivan, accessed September 19, 2017, http://www.heartofconeyisland.com/sea-lion-park-coney-island.html.

3. Christopher Klein, "Disneyland's Disastrous Opening Day," History.com, July 17, 2015, accessed September 19, 2017, http://www.history.com/news/disneylands-disastrous-opening-day-60-years-ago; Thomas Smith, "This Day in History: Walt Disney World Resort Officially Opens—1971," Disney Parks Blog, October 1, 2010, accessed September 19, 2017, https://disneyparks.disney.go.com/blog/2010/10/this-day-in-history-walt-disney-world-resort-officially-opens-1971/.

4. Lewis Howes, "20 Lessons from Walt Disney on Entrepreneurship, Innovation and Chasing Your Dreams," *Forbes*, July 17, 2012, accessed September 19, 2017, https://www.forbes.com/sites/lewishowes/2012/07/17/20-business-quotes-and-lessons-from-walt-disney/#63bfa0c4ba9a.

5. Victoria Messina, "18 Walt Disney Quotes That Will Inspire You to Chase Your Dreams," Allure Media, December 6, 2016, accessed September

19, 2017, https://www.popsugar.com.au/smart-living/Walt-Disney-Quotes -42806477#photo-42806476.

6. "Could Oswald the Lucky Rabbit Have Been Bigger Than Mickey?," BBC, December 3, 2012, accessed September 19, 2017, http://www.bbc .com/news/magazine-19910825.

7. "Walt Disney Acted Out Snow White and All Its Characters on Stage to Inspire His Team to Make the Movie," TheJournal.ie, September 27, 2015, accessed September 19, 2017, http://www.thejournal.ie/walt-disney -documentary-2343806-Sep2015/; "This Day in History, February 4, 1938: Disney Releases *Snow White and the Seven Dwarfs*," History.com, accessed September 19, 2017, http://www.history.com/this-day-in-history/disney -releases-snow-white-and-the-seven-dwarfs.

8. Andrea Patruno, "The Evolution of Animation," Luciscribia, March 11, 2016, accessed September 19, 2017, https://medium.com/luci-scribia/the -evolution-of-animation-5f12d55c7aa.

9. Diane Disney Miller, as told to Pete Martin, "Disney's Folly," *Saturday Evening Post*, accessed September 19, 2017, http://www .saturdayeveningpost.com/wp-content/uploads/satevepost/Disneys-Folly1.pdf.

10. Miller, "Disney's Folly."

11. Erin Glover, "Opening Night, 1937: 'Snow White and the Seven Dwarfs' Premieres at Carthay Circle Theatre," Disney Parks Blog, December 21, 2011, accessed September 19, 2017, https://disneyparks.disney .go.com/blog/2011/12/opening-night-1937-snow-white-and-the-seven-dwarfs -premieres-at-carthay-circle-theatre/.

12. Miller, "Disney's Folly."

13. "This Day in History, February 4, 1938."

14. "This Day in History, February 4, 1938."

15. Brian Galindo, "20 Fascinating Facts About 'Snow White and the Seven Dwarfs,'" BuzzFeed, April 18, 2013, accessed September 19, 2017, https://www.buzzfeed.com/briangalindo/20-fascinating-facts-about-snow -white-and-the-seven-dwarfs?utm_term=.bcEEyJlYY#.ml6vbO9GG.

16. Nathania Johnson, "Paralyzed Teen's Modeling Dream Comes True (and 4 More Inspiring Stories You Might Have Missed)," *People*, May 23, 2014, accessed September 19, 2017, http://people.com/human-interest /inspirational-good-news-paralyzed-teens-modeling-dreams-come-true/.

17. "Facts About Terry," Terry Fox Foundation, accessed September 14, 2017, http://www.terryfox.org/terrys-story/facts/.

18. Ken Stone, "Ida Keeling at 97 Becomes Oldest American Female Sprinter," *Masterstrack.com* (blog), June 11, 2012, accessed September 19, 2017, http://masterstrack.com/ida-keeling-at-97-becomes-oldest-american -female-sprinter/.

19. Jordan Jackson, "'Love Yourself!' Ida Keeling, 100, Explains How She Set a World Running Record," *TODAY*, May 5, 2016, https://www .today.com/health/love-yourself-ida-keeling-100-explains-how-she-set -world-t90721.

20. Napoleon Hill, *Think and Grow Rich* (Cleveland, OH: Ralston Publishing Co., 1953), 110.

DAY 6
TAKING THE LID OFF

1. Brian Tracy, as quoted on Quotefancy, accessed September 14, 2017, https://quotefancy.com/quote/777984/Brian-Tracy-You-begin-to-fly-when -you-let-go-of-self-limiting-beliefs-and-allow-your-mind.

2. "Astronaut Mae Jemison Launches Diversity Series With Message of Daring and Imagination," UVA Engineering, accessed September 14, 2017, http://enews.seas.virginia.edu/astronaut-mae-jemison-launches-diversity -series-with-message-of-daring-and-imagination/.

DAY 7
DROWNING DEATH-LACED WORDS

1. Mother Teresa, as quoted on BrainyQuote, accessed September 14, 2017, https://www.brainyquote.com/quotes/quotes/m/mothertere125705 .html.

DAY 8
FIGHTING FEAR'S FIERCE AGENDA

1. Fredd Culbertson, "The Phobia List," accessed September 14, 2017, http://phobialist.com/.

2. *Maury*, "I'm Scared to Death of Birds, Peaches & Pickles," Matthew Mcgrath's YouTube channel, May 21, 2010, https://www.youtube.com /watch?v=6q-SQtpjuYM; *Maury*, "We're Terrified of Flowers... Cotton...and Caterpillars!," ELTetlak's YouTube channel, August 6, 2009, https://www.youtube.com/watch?v=zOtkLmXxIG4.

3. Bible Hub, s.v. "*kathaireō*," accessed September 19, 2017, http:// biblehub.com/greek/2507.htm.

4. Blue Letter Bible, s.v. "*kathaireō*," accessed September 19, 2017, https://www.blueletterbible.org/lang/Lexicon/Lexicon.cfm?strongs =G2507&t=KJV.

5. Joyce Meyer, "Soar Like an Eagle," *Christian Post*, May 14, 2009, accessed September 19, 2017, http://www.christianpost.com/news/soar-like -an-eagle-38619/.

DAY 9
DISCONNECTING WRONG ALIGNMENTS

1. Kai Sato, "Why the Five People Around You Are Crucial to Your Success," *Entrepreneur*, May 9, 2014, accessed September 19, 2017, https://www.entrepreneur.com/article/233444.

2. Merriam-Webster, s.v. "suddenly," accessed September 14, 2017, https://www.merriam-webster.com/dictionary/suddenly.

3. *Encyclopedia of the Bible*, "John Mark," Bible Gateway, accessed September 14, 2017, https://www.biblegateway.com/resources /encyclopedia-of-the-bible/John-Mark.

4. George Washington, as quoted on Lifehack Quotes, accessed September 14, 2017, http://quotes.lifehack.org/quote/george-washington /it-is-better-to-be-alone-than/.

DAY 10
PRESSING PAST FAILURES

1. Henry Ford, as quoted in "People in the News," *Hope Star*, October 31, 1972, accessed September 17, 2017, https://www.newspapers.com /newspage/1586299/.

2. Newsweek Special Edition, "Michael Jordan Didn't Make Varsity—at First," *Newsweek*, October 17, 2015, accessed September 17, 2017, http://www.newsweek.com/missing-cut-382954/.

3. Nathan Furr, "How Failure Taught Edison to Repeatedly Innovate," *Forbes*, June 9, 2011, accessed September 17, 2017, https://www.forbes.com /sites/nathanfurr/2011/06/09/how-failure-taught-edison-to-repeatedly -innovate/#74337c5665e9.

4. Rachel Gillett, "How Walt Disney, Oprah Winfrey, and 19 Other Successful People Rebounded After Getting Fired," *Business Insider*, October 7, 2015, accessed September 17, 2017, https://www.inc.com /business-insider/21-successful-people-who-rebounded-after-getting-fired .html.

5. Gillett, "How Walt Disney, Oprah Winfrey, and 19 Other Successful People Rebounded After Getting Fired."

6. Les Brown, as quoted on Motivation, accessed September 14, 2017, http://www.motivation.com/quotes/188.

7. David McCullough, *Truman* (New York: Simon & Schuster, 1992), 141.

8. "Media Matters: Finest Hour 136, Autumn 2007," The International Churchill Society, accessed September 17, 2017, https://www .winstonchurchill.org/publications/finest-hour/finest-hour-136/media-matters.

DAY 11
FIGHTING OFF FRUSTRATIONS

1. *Merriam-Webster*, s.v. "frustration," accessed September 14, 2017, https://www.merriam-webster.com/dictionary/frustration.

2. *Strong's Exhaustive Concordance of the Bible*, s.v. "*charis*."

3. Dale Carnegie, *How to Stop Worrying and Start Living* (New York: Pocket Book, 1984), https://books.google.com/books?id=EVq1iCtj ZuAC&pg.

DAY 12
ROOTING OUT EVERY TRACE OF DOUBT

1. Kahlil Gibran, *The Kahlil Gibran Reader* (New York: Citadel Press, 1951, 1979), 36.

2. Fred Shapiro, "Quotes Uncovered: Honest Abe," Freakonomics (blog), May 3, 2011, http://freakonomics.com/2011/05/03/quotes-uncovered -honest-abe/.

3. *Merriam-Webster*, s.v. "shadow," accessed October 9, 2017, https:// www.merriam-webster.com/dictionary/shadow.

DAY 13
PRUNING IMPATIENCE

1. *Merriam-Webster*, s.v. "patient," accessed October 9, 2017, https:// www.merriam-webster.com/dictionary/patient.

2. Joyce Meyer, "When, God, When?" *Christian Post*, October 8, 2009, accessed October 9, 2017, http://www.christianpost.com/news/when-god -when-41307/.

3. *Merriam-Webster*, s.v. "impatient," accessed October 9, 2017, https:// www.merriam-webster.com/dictionary/impatient.

4. Martin Luther, *Commentary on Romans* (Grand Rapids, MI: Zondervan, 1954), 91.

5. Watchman Nee, *The Spiritual Man* (New York: Christian Fellowship Publishers, 2014), https://books.google.com/books?id=DcpOBAAA QBAJ&pg.

6. Oswald Chambers, *My Utmost for His Highest*, "The Patience of Faith," accessed October 9, 2017, https://utmost.org/classic/the-patience-of -faith-classic.

7. Ray Kroc, *Grinding It Out: The Making of McDonald's* (New York: St. Martin's Paperbacks, 1977), 201.

8. "Serenity Prayer – Applying 3 Truths from the Bible," Crosswalk.com, January 12, 2017, accessed October 9, 2017, http://www.crosswalk.com /faith/prayer/prayers/serenity-prayer-applying-3-truths-from-the-bible.html.

DAY 14
SLAMMING THE DOOR ON PROCRASTINATION

1. Jon R. Stone, *The Routledge Book of World Proverbs* (New York: Routledge, 2006), 435.

DAY 15
SENDING PERFECTIONISM PACKING

1. *Merriam-Webster,* s.v. "perfectionism," accessed September 7, 2017, https://www.merriam-webster.com/dictionary/perfectionism.

2. Vince Lombardi, as quoted on 247Sports, CBS Interactive, accessed September 14, 2017, http://247sports.com/Coach/3614/Quotes/Perfection-is -not-attainable-but-if-we-chase-perfection-we-can-c-35987460.

DAY 16
HEART ATTITUDES THAT HELP OR HINDER YOUR WILD DREAMS

1. "Biography," Viktor Frankl Institute, accessed October 10, 2017, http://www.viktorfrankl.org/e/chronology.html.

2. Viktor Frankl, *Man's Search for Meaning* (Boston: Beacon Press, 2006), 86.

3. Lynne Malcolm, "Scientific Evidence Points to Importance of Positive Thinking," June 17, 2015, accessed October 10, 2017, http://www.abc.net .au/radionational/programs/allinthemind/the-scientific-evidence-for-positive -thinking/6553614.

4. Michael Benson, *Winning Words* (Lanham, MD: Taylor Trade Publishing, 2008), 10.

DAY 17
LEAVING YOUR COMFORT ZONE

1. Alice Nash, "Richard Branson: How to Juggle Multiple Businesses," Virgin, July 24, 2014, accessed October 10, 2017, https://www.virgin.com /entrepreneur/richard-branson-how-juggle-multiple-businesses.

2. Nina Zipkin, "50 Inspirational Quotes to Help You Achieve Your Goals," *Entrepreneur,* February 2, 2017, accessed October 10, 2017, https:// www.entrepreneur.com/article/287870.

DAY 18
WEATHERING WILD ADVERSITY

1. Peter Nye, "Bald Eagle Characteristics," Journey North, accessed October 10, 2017, http://www.learner.org/jnorth/tm/eagle/facts _characteristics.html.

2. David Muturi, "Learn Eagle's Ways to Reach Great Heights of Success," Daily Nation, January 7, 2014, accessed October 10, 2017, http:// mobile.nation

.co.ke/lifestyle/eagle-success-Myles-Munroe/1950774-2367088-format-xhtml
-14ddk01/index.html.

3. Geoff Loftus, "If You're Going Through Hell, Keep Going—Winston Churchill," *Forbes*, May 9, 2012, accessed October 10, 2017, https://www .forbes.com/sites/geoffloftus/2012/05/09/if-youre-going-through-hell-keep -going-winston-churchill/#6439b6a4d549.

DAY 19
THE WAR AGAINST WEARINESS

1. Luis Palau, as quoted on Beliefnet, accessed October 11, 2017, http:// www.beliefnet.com/quotes/christian/l/luis-palau/when-you-face-the-perils-of -weariness-carelessnes.aspx.

DAY 20
PRAYING WITH PERSISTENCE

1. *Vine's Expository Dictionary of New Testament Words*, s.v. "knock," StudyLight.org, accessed October 11, 2017, http://studylight.org/dictionaries /ved/k/knock.html.

2. George Mueller, "Keep Asking," accessed October 11, 2017, http:// www.georgemuller.org/quotes/category/persistence.

DAY 21
THE BATTLE FOR FOCUS

1. Scott Koepf, "Don't Look at the Wall," travAlliancemedia, March 2016, http://www.travelpulse.com/articles/travel-agents/don-t-look-at-the -wall.html.

2. Zig Ziglar, "Lack of Direction," Ziglar, accessed October 12, 2017, https://www.ziglar.com/quotes/lack-of-direction/.

3. Bruce Lee, as quoted on Goodreads, accessed October 12, 2017, https://www.goodreads.com/quotes/461996-the-successful-warrior-is-the -average-man-with-laser-like-focus.

4. As quoted in Benny Kloth-Jorgensen, *Stepping Stones to Success* (N.p.: Athena Publishing, 2015), 69.

5. As quoted in Brett Willis, *Purposely Profitable* (Oxford, UK: John Wiley & Sons, Ltd., 2016), https://books.google.com/books/about /Purposely_Profitable.html?id=AeOeCwAAQBAJ.

6. This quote is widely circulated online. It is adapted from Ralph Waldo Emerson, *The Prose Works of Ralph Waldo Emerson* (Boston: James R. Osgood and Company, 1872), 353.

7. "In Quotes: Apple's Steve Jobs," BBC News, October 6, 2011, accessed October 12, 2017, http://www.bbc.co.uk/news/mobile/world-us -canada-15195448.

8. Steve Mueller, "The 30 Most Inspiring Focus Quotes," *Planet of Success* (blog), June 8, 2016, accessed November 2, 2017, http://www.planetofsuccess.com/blog/2016/inspiring-focus-quotes/.

9. For more time-tracking app options, see Cynthia Johnson, "8 Great Time-Tracking Apps for Freelancers," *Entrepreneur*, January 27, 2016, accessed October 12, 2017, https://www.entrepreneur.com/article/269991.

DAY 22
ASK GOD TO PUT HIS DESIRES IN YOUR HEART

1. *Vine's Expository Dictionary of New Testament Words*, s.v. "lust," accessed October 12, 2017, http://studybible.info/vines/Lust%20(Noun%20and%20Verb).

2. Rick Warren, "God Can Top Your Biggest Dream," Pastor Rick's Daily Hope, January 5, 2016, accessed October 12, 2017, http://pastorrick.com/devotional/english/full-post/god-can-top-your-biggest-dream.

3. Blue Letter Bible, s.v. "ʾanag," accessed October 12, 2017, https://www.blueletterbible.org/lang/Lexicon/Lexicon.cfm?strongs=H6026&t=KJV.

4. *Merriam-Webster*, s.v. "delight," accessed October 12, 2017, https://www.merriam-webster.com/dictionary/delight.

DAY 23
IMAGINE WHAT YOU WOULD DO WITH LIMITLESS MONEY

1. Wikipedia, "Fear, Uncertainty and Doubt," last updated September 3, 2017, accessed October 12, 2017, https://en.wikipedia.org/wiki/Fear,_uncertainty_and_doubt.

2. Blue Letter Bible, s.v. "koach," accessed October 12, 2017, https://www.blueletterbible.org/lang/Lexicon/Lexicon.cfm?strongs=H3581&t=KJV.

3. Blue Letter Bible, s.v. "ʾasah," accessed October 12, 2017, https://www.blueletterbible.org/lang/Lexicon/Lexicon.cfm?strongs=H6213&t=KJV; Blue Letter Bible, s.v. "chayil" accessed October 12, 2017, https://www.blueletterbible.org/lang/lexicon/lexicon.cfm?Strongs=H2428&t=KJV.

4. Rob Berger, "Top 100 Money Quotes of All Time," *Forbes*, April 30, 2014, accessed October 12, 2017, https://www.forbes.com/sites/robertberger/2014/04/30/top-100-money-quotes-of-all-time/#a80efab4998d.

DAY 24
WHAT IF YOU COULD NOT FAIL?

1. Ekaterina Walter, "30 Powerful Quotes on Failure," *Forbes*, December 30, 2013, accessed October 12, 2017, https://www.forbes.com/sites/ekaterinawalter/2013/12/30/30-powerful-quotes-on-failure/#4aa80ebc24bd.

2. Seth Poppel, "Michael Jordan Didn't Make Varsity—at First," *Newsweek Special Edition*, October 17, 2015, accessed October 12, 2017, http://www.newsweek.com/missing-cut-382954.

3. Poppel, "Michael Jordan Didn't Make Varsity—at First."

4. Poppel, "Michael Jordan Didn't Make Varsity—at First."

5. Poppel, "Michael Jordan Didn't Make Varsity—at First."

6. "How Many Has Michael Made?" NBA Media Ventures, LLC, accessed October 12, 2017, http://www.nba.com/jordan/game_winners .html.

7. Nike, "Failure," television advertisement, accessed October 12, 2017, viewed at https://www.youtube.com/watch?v=GuXZFQKKF7A.

8. Joel Siegel, "When Steve Jobs Got Fired by Apple," ABC News, October 6, 2011, accessed October 12, 2017, http://abcnews.go.com /Technology/steve-jobs-fire-company/story?id=14683754.

9. Paul Allen, "My Favorite Mistake: Paul Allen," *Newsweek*, April 24, 2011, accessed October 12, 2017, http://www.newsweek.com/my-favorite -mistake-paul-allen-66489.

10. "Celebs Who Went From Failures to Success Stories," CBS Interactive Inc., accessed October 12, 2017, https://www.cbsnews.com /pictures/celebs-who-went-from-failures-to-success-stories/3/; "Albert Einstein," A&E Television Networks, LLC, accessed October 12, 2017, https://www.biography.com/people/albert-einstein-9285408.

11. Your Dictionary, "Colonel Sanders Facts," accessed October 12, 2017, http://biography.yourdictionary.com/colonel-sanders.

12. Helene Panzarino, *Business Funding for Dummies* (Chichester, UK: John Wiley and Sons, 2016), 122.

13. "What Made Us Great Is Still What Makes Us Great," Kentucky Fried Chicken, accessed October 12, 2017, https://www.kfc.com/about.

14. Ekaterina Walter, "30 Powerful Quotes on Failure."

15. C. C. Holland, "10 Inspirations for Embracing Failure," CBS Interactive Inc., July 16, 2008, https://www.cbsnews.com/news/10 -inspirations-for-embracing-failure/.

16. Catherine Clifford, "10 Key Takeaways From the Book 'Shark Tank' Investor Daymond John Has Read 20 Times," CNBC, November 30, 2016, accessed October 12, 2017, https://www.cnbc.com/2016/11/30/10-key -takeaways-from-the-book-shark-tank-investor-daymond-john-has-read-20 -times.html.

17. Johnny Cash, Academy of Achievement interview, June 25, 1993, viewed on 20th Century Time Machine's YouTube channel, https://www .youtube.com/watch?v=s13eg4mWBnk.

18. Zig Ziglar, "How High You Bounce," Ziglar, May 26, 2015, accessed October 12, 2017, https://www.ziglar.com/quotes/its-not-how-far-you-fall/.

19. Kevin Kruse, "Zig Ziglar: 10 Quotes That Can Change Your Life," *Forbes*, November 28, 2012, accessed October 12, 2017, https://www.forbes

.com/sites/kevinkruse/2012/11/28/zig-ziglar-10-quotes-that-can-change-your
-life/#d77219826a0e.

DAY 25
WHAT IF YOU HAD NO FEARS?

1. As quoted in Joyce Meyer, *The Confident Woman* (Nashville, TN: FaithWords, 2006), https://books.google.com/books/about/The_Confident _Woman.html?id=5pNSQPiTGPsC.

DAY 26
WRITE THE VISION AND MAKE IT PLAIN

1. Helen Keller, as quoted on Values.com, accessed October 12, 2017, https://www.values.com/inspirational-quotes/7350-the-only-thing-worse -than-being-blind-is-having.

2. Amy Reid, "Myles Munroe: 'The Power of Vision,'" CBN, accessed October 12, 2017, http://www1.cbn.com/books/myles-munroe%3A-%27the -power-of-vision%27.

3. Charles Swindoll, "Optimism," Insight for Living Ministries, May 19, 2017, accessed October 12, 2017, https://www.insight.org/resources/daily -devotional/individual/optimism1.

4. James Allen, *As a Man Thinketh* (Seattle, WA: Pacific Publishing Studio, 2009), 43, https://www.amazon.com/As-Man-Thinketh-James-Allen /dp/0982445482/ref=tmm_pap_title_6?_encoding=UTF8&qid=&sr=.

5. Henry David Thoreau, *Walden* (New York: Thomas Y. Crowell, 1910), 427, https://books.google.com/books?id=yiQ3AAAAIAAJ.

6. Gregory M. Lamb, "11 Quotes From Difference Makers," *Christian Science Monitor*, February 28, 2013, accessed October 12, 2017, https:// www.csmonitor.com/World/Making-a-difference/2013/0228/11-quotes -from-difference-makers/Leonardo-da-Vinci.

7. "The Magic of Thinking Big—27 Quotes That Will Change Your Life," The Inspiring Journal, July 31, 2015, accessed October 12, 2017, http://www.theinspiringjournal.com/the-magic-of-thinking-big-27-quotes -that-will-change-your-life/.

8. Andy Stanley, *Making Vision Stick* (Grand Rapids, MI: Zondervan, 2007), 33.

9. Beth Darlington, ed., *The Love Letters of William and Mary Wordsworth* (Ithaca, NY: Cornell University Press, 1981), 112.

10. Billy Graham, "We Still Worship 'Idols' Like Money, Power and Possessions," *Chicago Tribune*, April 25, 2012, accessed October 12, 2017, http://articles.chicagotribune.com/2012-04-25/features/sns-201204030000 —tms—bgrahamctnym-a20120425apr25_1_idols-worship-god.

11. Andrew Murray, as quoted on Beliefnet, accessed October 12, 2017, http://www.beliefnet.com/quotes/evangelical/a/andrew-murray/prayer-is-not -monologue-but-dialogue-gods-voice.aspx.

12. John C. Maxwell, "The Seven Demands of Leadership," *Christian Post*, March 19, 2007, accessed October 12, 2017, http://www.christianpost .com/news/the-seven-demands-of-leadership-26410/.

DAY 27
CREATE A SPIRIT-LED PLAN

1. "Famous Pablo Picasso Quotes," www.PabloPicasso.org, accessed October 12, 2017, https://www.pablopicasso.org/quotes.jsp.

2. "7 Must Read Life Lessons from Benjamin Franklin," Business Insider Inc., May 31, 2011, accessed October 12, 2017, http://www .businessinsider.com/7-must-read-life-lessons-from-benjamin-franklin-2011-6.

3. Hana Bieliauskas, "6 Abraham Lincoln Quotes to Inspire Communicators," Ragan Communications Inc., December 30, 2013, accessed October 12, 2017, https://www.prdaily.com/Main/Articles/6 _Abraham_Lincoln_quotes_to_inspire_communicators_13827.aspx.

4. Michele Gorman, "Yogi Berra's Most Memorable Sayings," *Newsweek*, September 23, 2015, accessed October 12, 2017, http://www.newsweek.com /most-memorable-yogi-isms-375661.

5. As quoted in Elizabeth Gilbert, *Big Magic* (New York: Riverhead Books, 2015), 177.

6. As quoted in Richard Nixon, *Six Crises* (New York: Doubleday, 1962), 235, https://www.amazon.com/Six-Crises-Richard-M-Nixon /dp/4871877639.

7. Blue Letter Bible, s.v. "*kakōs*," accessed October 12, 2017, https:// www.blueletterbible.org/lang/Lexicon/Lexicon.cfm?strongs=G2560&t=KJV.

DAY 28
WRITE OUT ACTIONABLE GOALS

1. Wikipedia, "SMART Criteria," last updated August 7, 2017, https:// en.wikipedia.org/wiki/SMART_criteria.

2. Kevin Kruse, "Zig Ziglar: 10 Quotes That Can Change Your Life."

DAY 29
TAKE CONSISTENT ACTION

1. *Merriam-Webster*, s.v. "faith," accessed October 12, 2017, https://www .merriam-webster.com/dictionary/faith.

2. Jim Rohn, "Rohn: 4 Straightforward Steps to Success," *SUCCESS*, March 31, 2015, accessed October 12, 2017, http://www.success.com/article /rohn-4-straightforward-steps-to-success.

3. *Merriam-Webster*, s.v. "consistent," accessed October 12, 2017, https://www.merriam-webster.com/dictionary/consistent.

4. *Merriam-Webster*, s.v. "inconsistent," accessed October 12, 2017, https://www.merriam-webster.com/dictionary/inconsistent.

5. Blue Letter Bible, s.v. "*egkrateia*," accessed October 12, 2017, https://www.blueletterbible.org/lang/Lexicon/Lexicon.cfm?strongs=G1466&t=KJV.

6. Charles R. Swindoll, *Growing Strong in the Seasons of Life* (Grand Rapids, MI: Zondervan, 2007), 24–25.

7. Robert C. Jameson, "Careful of Your Thoughts: They Control Your Destiny," Oath Inc., June 28, 2014, accessed October 12, 2017, http://www.huffingtonpost.com/robert-c-jameson/be-careful-of-your-though_b_5214689.html.

DAY 30
ASK, ASK, ASK

1. Mitzi Weinman, *It's About Time!* (Bloomington, IN: iUniverse, 2014), 61.